Praise for *Pa*

Fantastic book, helped create a more peaceful environment to live in!

-Amanda Catarzi, Author of
Subconsciously Conscious

I started reading this book to support the author and didn't expect to get much out of it because I didn't consider myself to be a packrat. I was completely wrong. This book challenged me to clean up my house. I started small (as she suggests in the book) and have been going room by room ever since. Now **I've made hundreds of dollars selling things I've decluttered.** I am preparing for a big move and I know there will be way less boxes in the truck when we pack it thanks to this book!

-Nick Spindler, *Blogger Speaker Podcaster*
iamnickspindler.com

This book was POWERFUL! Not only did I learn practical tips on how to eliminate the unnecessary clutter in my life but it also equipped me with the tools to KEEP the clutter out!

-Heather Parady, Host of the
Unconventional Leaders Podcast

One of my favorite things about this book is that it's not scary. And it's not a massive, overwhelming tome of do's and don't's. Instead it is a short, easy read, includes firsthand accounts from recovering packrats as well as tons of encouragement and nuggets of wisdom designed to help the reader develop a positive mindset about decluttering. Getting your mind right is a big part of the battle.

-Stephanie Bain, Author of *The Girl I Left Behind*

Amazon Reviews
of *Packrat to Clutter-Free*

If you have read Marie Kondo's book and thought it a bit too extreme, **this book is the one for you** I think. It's a more realistic take on de-cluttering and organization, in easy to read language.

– Robert

My clutter was taking over and I had no idea where to start. This book took the stress of wondering where to begin away and broke things down into easily managed steps for each room/section of the house. So far, **I've thrown away or donated 60 bags of stuff.** That's 60 bags of stuff no longer in my house!

– Shannon

This book is amazing for those of us who tend to be scattered!

– Jenny

I would highly recommend to anyone wishing to get rid of clutter in any aspect of their life. From home to car to children even organizing your recipes. **Megan even has a touch of humor** in her book. Very good read!

– Barbara

Packrat
to
Clutter-Free

M. C. Starbuck

for Momsy

who taught me to value people over possessions

CONTENTS

One

BEFORE & AFTER
A Typical Day in the Life of a Packrat

"Isn't it funny how day by day
nothing changes, but when you look back,
everything is different?"
- C. S. Lewis

She opens her eyes to a sea of busyness. Small knick knacks fill every surface. Clothes cover the floor, and books are in piles because there's no more room on the shelves. She's used to navigating the maze on her way to the bathroom. As she washes her hands, items fall into the sink or onto the floor.

She bends in frustration to pick them up and return them to their place on the crowded counter, knowing it's only a matter of time before they fall again. Tomorrow she may not even bother picking them up.

She kicks her shoes out of the way as she walks to the closet to find an outfit for the day. She grabs whatever's most accessible. Even then, she has to tug and shift to get the clothes free. Her arm bumps the closet door as she gets dressed in the crowded room. She looks in the mirror, stressed by the unfinished project she sees in the background.

The clothes don't do anything to lift her mood. There's a small stain she'd forgotten about, and it never fit just right anyway. But it'll do. She shuffles around to find her purse, then heaves it onto her shoulder. It's weight digs in as she trudges to the car where she plops it down onto the passenger's seat.

Her eye catches the backseat, and she remembers she needs to unpack from her trip last week. No time for that now.

That evening, the pile of mail on the counter taunts her. What a welcome home. She retreats to the couch where she stares at her phone to gain a sense of freedom and productivity. The laundry can wait. She can hardly open the door to get in there anyway.

There's a knock on the door.

"Sarah! Hey...you know you're truly my friend if I'm letting you in this mess!"

"Oh, I'm not staying anyway. I just wanted to return this dish. Thank you so much for the meal a couple of weeks ago. Sorry I'm just now getting this back to you."

"Okay, thank you! See you later!"

Alone again, she takes the clean casserole dish and fights to shimmy it into a cabinet, making quite the racket as she goes. She feels like she just did a 20-minute workout by the time she's done.

That evening she gathers piles of work from her bed and tosses them to the floor and a nearby chair. She crawls into bed drained. She turns on the lamp to read. Everything else disappears in the darkness, but she knows it's still there to greet her in the morning.

A Day in a Clutter-Free Life

She wakes up to the sunlight shining on her bed.

Once again, she notices how cute her dresser is with a bouquet of flowers, a framed photo of her loved ones, a candle, and her favorite journal.

She walks to the bathroom and washes her face in peace—there's so much counter space. Once she gets to the closet, she can't decide what to wear—she loves it all! She chooses a simple dress and is pleased when she checks the mirror.

She grabs her purse from the basket by the door where she almost always leaves it. Even full, it still zips shut. It holds all the essentials for such a small bag. It's so lightweight that it doesn't weigh her down.

She walks to her car, one that passengers could actually fit into, and goes on with her day.

When Sarah stops by that evening, she is welcomed inside and accepts an offer of tea. The two of them have a nice chat in the peaceful living room before Sarah has to leave.

Alone again, she puts everything from supper away quickly so she can move on to working on her latest project.

At night, she crawls into bed, ready to do it all over again. She didn't finish everything on her list, but that just gives her something to be excited for tomorrow.

Day 1
5-minute Task
Take detailed Before pictures. I get tired of saying this, but don't skip this step! Even though I say it, people still come to me saying, "I wish I'd taken a Before picture, but look at the After!" Don't let that be you. This step is easy. If you can't do this one, how will you do the others?

I'm intentional in saying to take *detailed* pictures. Take pictures inside of drawers and cabinets. Take pictures of individual shelves. Then it will be faster and easier to get an After photo.

Go ahead and snap those pictures in *every* room of your house. I've thought so many times, "Oh, I'm not working on that area, so I don't need a picture now." But once I get going with decluttering, I'm not going to stop in the middle to take a picture before I place one item where it goes. Yet one item here, and one item there, really adds up.

Pro tip: It helps if you line the picture up with a doorway or window or something to serve as a frame of reference. Then when you take your After pictures, you'll be able to line it up at the same spot for a better comparison.

Two

UNHINDERED
Clearing the Clutter that Keeps You Distracted

"That which hinders your task is your task."
- Sanford Meisner

What kind of life do you want to live?

Seems like a heavy question for something as surface-level as learning to manage your possessions. But what's the point of decluttering if it doesn't improve our lives? When I started decluttering, I thought the point was so I could live in a tiny house without tripping over stuff. What I've since found is that being clutter-free keeps me from being held back from pursuing dreams I've been called to walk in.

I had to literally clear the path to becoming an author and even a wife.

So, what kind of life do you want?

Do you want to stop living in fear of inviting people over because you don't want them to see the chaos of your home? Raise your hand if you know someone whose house appears spotless but who still apologizes for the mess. I hate to break it to you, but you can be miserable even with a perfectly clean home. You can also be happy even in a messy home. However, that doesn't mean you should *try* to have a messy house.

When your possessions have become an inconvenience, when managing them has taken over your life, when you're tired of shuffling your belongings around and feeling like you're getting nowhere, that's when you're ready for a clutter-free life. When your clutter is preventing you from accomplishing what you set out to do, that's when it's time to declutter. **You are ready to begin when you've stopped thinking you don't have time to declutter and instead believe you don't have time *not* to.**

What is your clutter keeping you from doing?

What would you love to do, but when you see all the "stuff," you just get too tired? Would you exercise more if there were space in the living room? Would you cook for your family more if the dishes weren't always piled up?

Would you pursue writing a book if you weren't so distracted by things you have to take care of? Would you start a small group, or even just invite people over, if you weren't embarrassed by your home? Would you talk to your kids more if you didn't feel like you needed to be on your phone to avoid the mess stressing you out?

Would you adopt a child, start a business, plant a garden, plant a church, go to college? Would you plan a road trip or travel overseas? Start a band? Pitch a song you wrote? Start a YouTube channel or a podcast? If you just had some breathing room in your life, what would you do with it?

Whatever your desire, if the clutter is hindering it, then decluttering will clear the path to it. You will still have to walk the rest of the path towards it after you declutter, but it will be faster or easier or more straightforward once the clutter is out of the way.

Can you still reach goals with a cluttered house? Certainly! People do it every day. In fact, my first big goal was to pay off $25k in student loans. And I did that *before* I started decluttering. Even though I'm clutter-free now, I find myself wondering why I still can't accomplish everything I set out to do from day to day. But if you're like me, you will look back year after year and be amazed at how different your life is once you go from being a packrat to being clutter-free.

Becoming clutter-free will even clear the way for opportunities you don't yet know about. I didn't set out with decluttering so I could publish a book about it. I knew I wanted to write a book, but I didn't have an idea for one. I also wasn't decluttering to make room in my life for marriage. Yet the short story is that that's exactly what happened. Of course other things played a role as well, but being clutter-free was no small part since I married a man whose job requires frequent moves. I didn't know that would happen. I wouldn't even know he existed until a full year *after* I *finished* my six months of decluttering.

Knowing what being clutter-free is making room for will not only keep you going throughout the decluttering process, but it will also help you know what items to keep. People often say to let go of anything you haven't used in the last year, but that never fully made sense to me. What if I haven't worked on my goal in the last year because my clutter was in the way? What if your exercise equipment went unused because it was hidden beneath a pile of clothes?

If your goal is to exercise more, you might want to keep the equipment and see if you use it once it isn't lost in the chaos. Those weights sitting out can be a daily reminder of your goal. Knowing your next goal will also help you see what to get rid of. I had a collection of yarn because I enjoy crocheting. I found balls of yarn for twenty-five cents each. What a steal! But as I was decluttering, I realized I had this huge pile of yarn taking up a significant portion of my space even though I wanted it to only take up a small amount of my time.

I knew I wanted writing a book to be my primary creative outlet, so I kept a small basket of yarn. I got rid of the rest and haven't missed it. Plus, the tiny basket is so cozy and adorable compared to the out-of-control and overflowing bags I kept all the other yarn in.

I don't want to live the life of a crafter, unless that craft is writing. That doesn't mean I can't ever paint or work on a project other than a book. It just means I don't keep as extensive of a collection as someone who crafts for a living or as a side job.

It means I'm not distracted from my true calling because of the craft supplies I feel obligated to use. Instead, I have a few basic art supplies that are there for me when I want a break from my work. Then I can go back to my writing refreshed and inspired. My craft projects are no longer scattered all over the house. My writing projects are instead. But that's okay. That's what I want to be "distracted" by. I want my writing to call my name and get my attention daily. That's *my* goal and *my* focus. What's yours?

Day 2
5-minute Task
Write down your goal. Not your goal for decluttering—your goal of what you will be able to do better once your clutter is no longer a hindrance. You can probably do this one in *less* than 5 minutes!

Three

DECLUTTERING VS. ORGANIZING

"Embrace the glorious mess that you are."
- Elizabeth Gilbert

My free spirit has never been drawn to books about decluttering or even organizing. Growing up, I liked to organize *occasionally*, but I just did it however I wanted—using whatever method made sense to me at the time.

Before I go any further, let me first clarify that when I talk about decluttering, I don't mean making an area *look* less cluttered. I don't mean "hiding" the clutter behind a door. I mean getting it out of the house. Even when my house doesn't look less cluttered, I still feel less weight from all my possessions because I know that the drawers and cabinets aren't in as much chaos as before.

While I have changed many of my mindsets and actions since I started this journey of going from packrat to clutter-free, I have not changed my values or completely done away with my messy creative side. I'm still the same free spirit I've always been. **I want others like me to know it's possible to make this transition while still maintaining a zest for life. If anything, my zest for life has grown.**

As I looked into downsizing and tiny houses, one thing I wasn't excited about was minimalism and how often it kept coming up. I've had mixed feelings about the term, so let's take a look at how Merriam-Webster defines it.

Minimalism: "style that is characterized by extreme spareness and simplicity."

For so long, I believed that minimalism was bland and sterile or even just too sophisticated, which isn't how I'd describe myself. I'm glad I found out I was wrong about minimalism.

In regards to the amount of possessions we own, I like to think of minimalism as being closer to a hotel room than many of the houses we live in today. Some people may have even less furniture than a hotel, but most of us have more. Yet hotel rooms can vary greatly in their style and design while having many similarities in the amount of items they contain. And I don't know about you, but when I walk into a hotel room, I'm usually not thinking, "Man, I wish this place had more stuff in it." Rather, I'm thinking, "Ahh, this is so peaceful and just right for my needs." That's how I want to feel when I walk into my home.

I'm also usually not thinking that a hotel is bland. I might not like all the furniture or decor, but it usually isn't bad. Even if I reduce the number of items I own down to the amount that makes each room feel more like a hotel, the feel of my house will still be different and will reflect different needs and tastes. It will still be my own possessions that remain, not someone else's. And there can be a difference in the style even from room to room in my own house if I so choose. Minimalism isn't a cookie cutter style.

Minimalism is up to the person creating the lifestyle. It can be plain or it can be colorful. It can be extreme or it can be practical.

Your Dream Hotel

Imagine with me what your dream hotel would look like. How would you choose to have it decorated? Visualize it without all your possessions inside—just the primary décor if you didn't live there. If it were a place you only visited, how would it feel when you walk in? What would it inspire you and other guests to do? Who would be drawn to your hotel? Who would feel welcome there?

I imagine a light, airy space with lots of clean white yet accents of pink, gold, and slate. It would be relaxing and inspiring. I'd feel like I have room to breathe, focus, and create. I would believe I could be productive and enjoy conversations because I'm not worried about anything extra. In Megan's Hotel, there would be time to write, dream, connect, plan, and pursue what's most important in life. Don't forget a splash of fun!

Doesn't that sound wonderful to have your own personalized hotel?

But that's kind of what our homes are. It doesn't always seem like it, but that's because we don't think of it that way. Therefore we don't set it up that way. Maybe we don't have room service or a cleaning staff, but could it be because that isn't our priority? If we really wanted that, couldn't we put all of our resources towards hiring someone for those services? Even if we can't afford it at the moment, we could save up and work towards it until we *could* afford it if that was really our goal in life.

If we make having a clutter-free home our goal for a season, our house can begin to look and feel more and more like a hotel even without those services. Our homes are temporary. Sure, we stay in them longer than we stay in a hotel, but when we realize they are not eternal, then we can see that they are just another tool.

Our homes have a purpose. What's the purpose of yours? To provide protection? To give you a place to gather? A place to eat and sleep? Is it a hub for you to run your business or fulfill your calling? A place to entertain and be entertained? It sounds a lot like a hotel to me.

So why do we allow so much extra that distracts us from using our homes for the purposes we desire to use it for? Why do we treat our homes like storage facilities rather than places to *live*?

Decluttering for Packrats

Here I am writing a book about how I decluttered (though not quite to the point of minimalism yet), and I'm hoping that people who aren't drawn to books about decluttering will somehow be drawn to this one.

Even though it seems crazy, I'm doing it because I believe you'll find value in my story in a way that can change your lives as it has changed mine. This book isn't just tips and tricks to help people declutter.

It's mostly just my *story* of how I went from being a packrat to where I am now, which does include lots of ideas to help you become clutter-free. This state of being clutter-free will look different for everyone, but the biggest difference will be in how it *feels*.

For me, it wasn't the *strategies* that people shared that got me excited about getting rid of clutter to begin with. It was their *stories*.

I'm not writing this book to paint the picture that my life is perfect and that decluttering fixes everything, but my life *is* better now. There's no going back, and not even a desire to. It's a small part of my life, but having it under control does allow me to enjoy everything else more and move on to improving other areas of my life. I wrote the first chapter about the typical day in the life of a packrat from personal experience, but I also wrote about a day in a clutter-free life from my own experience.

While my house may still look cluttered to others, to me it *feels* clutter-free compared to how it was before I started getting rid of stuff. Even more than that, *I* feel clutter-free. And much of that state of feeling clutter-free has to do with the fact that I can manage all my possessions. Piles of paper aren't overflowing every surface and keeping me distracted. When they *do* start to pile up, they annoy me sooner so I can deal with them before they're too overwhelming. Plus, I know *how* to deal with them now. Boxes of unknown contents aren't lining every wall and weighing on me while I'm trying to complete some other task. I know where items are when I need them. I'm able to focus on what I'm doing, and for the most part, things are functioning the way I want them to. I no longer identify as a packrat. I don't *think* like one, nor do I *act* like one…most of the time.

I read blogs about how decluttering changed their lives for the better. I watched videos about how it brought them closer to their families. I listened to podcasts about how they downsized so they could travel. And I heard speakers share how it gave them freedom to pursue their dreams and how it filled them with purpose that helped them focus on what matters to them.

A clutter-free house wasn't exactly on my bucket list, but *those other things were*. Their joy and contentment and simple lives inspired me to change and motivated me to keep learning about how to become clutter-free.

I hope my story does the same for you.

Day 3

5-min Task

Create a Donation Station—an area everyone in the home knows they can put items they no longer want. You may need to make it clear that they are to only place their own items in this bin. You can use a box or a bag, but I like including a bin as well so that when I take the bag for donation, the bin is still there, and I don't have to set up the Donation Station again every time.

Four

THE DANGER OF CLUTTER

"One can furnish a room very luxuriously by taking out
furniture rather than putting it in."
- Francis Jourdain,

Furniture Maker/Interior Designer

I'm not one to be overly dramatic, so I'll go ahead and say that
clutter hasn't caused any deaths or serious injuries in my family.
We've had lots of stuff packed into small areas, which means we got
good at stepping over and maneuvering around the numerous piles
scattered throughout the house.

But let me just say, I have seen a few boxes fall from a closet onto
someone's head.

It really can be dangerous, especially for older people or young
children, to have stacks of boxes everywhere. Stubbed toes,
difficulty navigating a room, or tripping over obstacles can all
unnecessarily add extra discomfort and inconvenience to each day.

While we haven't had our house catch on fire, it could be quite the task to escape from a window in certain rooms or for someone to try to rescue us.

The possibility of injuries is certainly something to keep in mind.

The most common danger of living with clutter, though, is how it slowly keeps building up over time. It's barely noticeable because of how gradual it is, but it eventually had a huge effect on my mind. I started getting frustrated without even realizing that it was because of the clutter in the way of everything I was trying to do. Plus, it was always on my mental to-do list to put away any items that were on the floor. Yet sometimes those items didn't have anywhere to go because my room was so packed full of stuff already.

How I Realized I Had a Problem

One day after I'd returned from a tiny house workshop, my younger brother suggested that I measure my current living space. It seemed logical. The idea was that doing so would help me realize how many square feet I should account for in the tiny house so that I could see if all my stuff would fit into it. I had no problem doing this because of course it would all fit! Au contraire. If I had put all my stuff in a tiny house, there would've been no room left for *me*.

Around the time he gave me that idea, though, I read a few articles about downsizing and decluttering. The more complicated my life felt, the more peaceful I wanted it to be.

Real people, in the tiny house community I was researching so much, were talking about how they were able to let go of things they once thought they needed...and how freeing it was.

As a packrat, this was foreign to me. Hearing about it really changed my life.

My original plan was to build a tiny house and move only the items that I really used or that were most important to me. Then I would get rid of the rest.

Measuring my room made me realize the problem: my tiny house was a year or two away. Since the room I was living in at the time was about the size of a tiny house, I had to face the fact that my future tiny house wouldn't end up looking much different than my room. And, unfortunately, my room always felt like an overcrowded disaster—even after I'd spent hours cleaning and organizing.

I wanted to enjoy freedom from material possessions immediately and not wait until my tiny house was built in order to enjoy that freedom. So I began the process.

Once I started getting rid of stuff, the freedom I began to feel was such a great experience that I wrote a blog post about it. I shared how I was able to overcome some of my hoarding tendencies (more about that in a later chapter).

I'm still in the process of giving stuff away, thanks to all the blog posts I read that got me started. That's what I love about downsizing, or as I like to call it, living tiny. You can start right away, and you can continue finding ways to improve for years. There are endless ways to live tiny, even in our culture, which has us trained to live big. Living big is not the norm for all cultures. It's been very eye-opening for me to travel to different countries and see how people in those communities live with less space and fewer possessions.

Because I'd been a packrat for decades, I had a long way to go in my journey. But as I slowly began getting rid of stuff in preparation for moving into a tiny house, I realized that I felt like I had already started living tiny.

Even though I didn't have my tiny house yet, it had already improved my life. Instead of defining living tiny as a certain square footage, I wrote out my own basic definition.

Living tiny: freeing oneself from excess and waste; simplifying

By that definition, anyone can live tiny.

And I don't mean getting rid of all excess. I love when people can afford a big house and use the space for more than just protecting stuff they rarely use. I have friends and family with a passion and talent for opening their homes to guests or using their space to create amazing works of art or businesses that are helping change people's lives.

I myself haven't even yet owned a tiny house and, due to life circumstances, no longer have a need to. But the decision to go ahead and live tiny has made my new living situation exciting instead of an obstacle to my dreams. I'm not having to put my goals on hold while I figure out what to do with all my stuff. I've already gotten rid of most of it, so I'm not having to continue taking care of it.

I remember watching the documentary *Tiny: A Story about Living Small*, and thinking this statement in it was so profound:

> "My ideal house is one where the outside draws you
> in and the inside draws you out."

I'm so glad that statement can apply to houses larger than 600 sq. ft, too. Tiny living still makes so much sense to me because I hate wasting everything from opportunities and space to time and money.

Having lots of stuff can really take a toll on those last two. It seems like we all think it would be nice to have a housekeeper take care of making everything look tidy, but there are so many other things we'd rather budget that money for.

Even with a housekeeper, my house would've still been a mess. It would've been a clean, organized mess. But it still would've been overwhelming and busy rather than relaxing and calm. It still would have been a danger zone. So I had to teach myself how to change that.

Day 4
5-min Task
Track your progress. Put a sheet of stickers by the bin so you can add one every time you donate a bag, or mark an x on a chart you keep at your Donation Station for every box of stuff you declutter. This will sustain you on the days you feel like you've done so much work but have nothing to show for it because your house still looks cluttered.

Five

NEEDING MORE THAN A HOUSEKEEPER

"I don't like the terms 'housewife' and 'homemaker;'
I prefer to be called 'Domestic Goddess'
… it's more descriptive."
- Roseanne Barr

The internet is full of ideas about how to organize clutter. I feel like I've tried them all and then some. My upbringing provided me with a few different ways of dealing with clutter, or *hiding* it.

We never had a housekeeper growing up, so it was easy to think having one would solve all of our clutter problems. As a nanny in a house where they had a housekeeper, I was able to see that more goes into solving clutter problems than having a housekeeper.

The housekeeper didn't throw away the family's belongings or make piles of items to be donated. She didn't even always put items where they go. The housekeeper's job was to make sure things were clean. That meant she piled papers in a neat stack, but she didn't sort through them or file them away. She might gather toys that were strewn across the floor and put them in a pile so she could vacuum, but they could be scattered by the children again within fifteen minutes.

Needing More Than a Housekeeper

Having a housekeeper didn't mean the family never cleaned. In fact, it meant they tidied up more often. They got the house prepped before the housekeeper arrived to clean every other week. And my friends who had cleaning ladies while growing up have also attested to this fact. Having a housekeeper does not reduce the amount of tidying necessary, but decluttering does.

In trying different methods of dealing with my possessions, I learned that there is more than one wrong way to handle clutter. And I've probably done them all. For a long time, I simply embraced or ignored the chaos because I thought there was no way to get rid of it.

Even when I realized I wanted to get rid of clutter, I would start to organize it or sort through one area all day long, only to find everywhere else had gotten more disastrous. After a few weeks, I was right back where I started.

Below is a list of common suggestions found in magazines and online. These are the things I was told would help make the clutter more manageable.

I tried every one of them:

- getting rid of 3-5 items a day
- organizing all the stuff in one area
- cleaning all day long
- sorting through one box at a time
- getting rid of one or two items every time I got a new item
- donating stuff I hadn't used in six months to a year

While those ideas can be helpful when added to an overall plan or when maintaining a space that's already clutter-free, they weren't enough for me to see any progress without additional strategies. None of them worked because I had too much stuff.

What's the strategy for people like me who could get rid of three items a day for two years and still have clutter? What if I see value in everything I have, and therefore find it difficult to part with anything?

I wish I had known a long time ago that "getting rid of clutter would eliminate 40% of housework in the average home." Thank you, National Soap and Detergent Association, for that nifty fact!

When I began my quest to live tiny, I was in a very active Facebook group where author and speaker Jon Acuff encouraged members to set goals, one month at a time. That group influenced my plan to get rid of enough stuff so I could fit everything I own into a tiny house. Even though I knew I couldn't declutter everything I own in only one month, I realized I could do it in six months if I focused on one aspect per month.

Part of why this plan works is because it's flexible and simple. I adjusted it to fit my life at the time. Because I'd paid off my student loans and didn't have many bills, I was able to clear out my schedule so I could spend a lot of time at home during those six months. I did still travel, but before I left and after I returned, I made sure to focus on getting rid of clutter. That doesn't mean I spent all day decluttering even when I was home. Being at home more consistently allowed me to take care of tasks on my to-do list and still have time to get rid of my clutter. I couldn't have done that if I wasn't home.

If you decluttered for an average of 30 minutes a day for six months, that would total 90 hours of decluttering. Because it's an average, some days you might declutter for an hour, but for other days you won't have to declutter at all—and you'll still make it to 90 hours! You might not even need 90 hours total. Maybe you could have it done in 45, which means you only need 15 minutes a day for six months or 30 minutes a day for three months. The point is that you can adjust it to what works for you, so that you can be clutter-free in your own timing.

For a thorough decluttering, I needed an end goal to keep me on track and help me not get discouraged thinking decluttering is a never-ending project. Having started in January, I decided to try (and was able) to finish by the 4th of July. As a client of mine who joined me in this endeavor pointed out, we were then able to celebrate our freedom from clutter along with our independence as a country!

Once I had the end in mind, I was able to come up with a plan. **Sometimes when I hear the word "plan" my free spirit slumps a little,** but coming up with my decluttering plan was actually freeing and fun. **It was a relief to know exactly what I was going to be doing and that I wasn't leaving anything out.** That plan allowed me to focus only on what I was supposed to be doing for a certain month. I didn't get a housekeeper, but I did kinda feel like a domestic goddess once I started implementing this plan.

Day 5
5-min Task
Go from room to room collecting the most obvious items to get rid of quickly and easily—even if it's literally just trash at this point. This is not the time to sit down with a box of stuff to sort through. This is the time to show yourself how much you can do in a small amount of time.

Six

HOARDING WAS MY LOVE LANGUAGE

"Years from now,
when all the junk they got is broken and long forgotten,
you'll still have your stars."
- Jeannette Walls

While working at a camp in Texas, my Secret Santa kept having people ask me for a list of my favorite things. At the end of the exhausting week of eating cafeteria food, on my bed waiting for me was a pile of my go-to snacks along with a note. I love food and letters anyway, so it was an extra awesome gift. I felt like I'd been visited by my mom, which also meant a lot because she was a 15-hour drive away. Working at Camp Summit was the first time I'd lived more than an hour and a half from where I was born and raised.

After hearing that story, it isn't hard to believe that receiving gifts and words of affirmation are my love languages. Thankfully I was able to eat those snacks and they no longer took up any space.

Hoarding was My Love Language

In her memoir *The Glass Castle*, Jeannette Walls shares the story of her dad telling his kids to pick out a star from the sky for Christmas because they couldn't afford anything else. I love the point he makes when he tells them that the toys other kids were getting could end up broken or forgotten. For them, the gift of a star was an experience. Good memories can be made with intangible gifts, too. And the memories made with tangible gifts can still remain even after the gift is gone.

Before I changed my way of thinking, having gifts and words of affirmations as two of my top love languages translated into wanting to keep every gift and note ever given to me. But these gifts don't disappear like food or stay in the sky like stars. I still have six boxes of letters written to me over the years. I've been able to part with the ones from my childhood that were from people I haven't stayed in touch with as much. The others are still a great source of joy, although I do intend to go through them later to see if there are any I'm okay with giving up.

But before I learned to get rid of stuff, I collected it from everyone I loved.

My sister, whom I dearly love, passed whatever she didn't want down to me while we were growing up. She's 8 years older, so I admired what she had and treasured it once I got to have it as my own.

My grandparents all passed away while I was in college. I always had the best time with them, so of course I was eager to keep what they had surrounded themselves with through the years. I couldn't comprehend why no one else would want it. I carried out stacks of books, boxes of dishes, and furniture for my future home.

I had no idea that I wouldn't need dishes or furniture of my own for the next 7 years. So I piled my stuff up at my mom's, my dad's, and my sister's houses while I just took what would fit in my car with me. For a while there was even stuff at my brother's and grandma's.

As I accumulated more over the years, I subconsciously tried to justify it by telling myself: "It's not *my* fault I love people and actually care about what they give me and things that remind me of them. That's not a bad thing!"

It looked like hoarding was just my love language, and there was no changing it.

As I'd watch my favorite Christmas movie, *How the Grinch Stole Christmas*, I always thought it such a shame when he talked about how the Who's gifts would just end up in the garbage. Who would do that?!

Apparently people who don't want lots of clutter.

I prefer to donate rather than throw away gifts, which still causes a problem when it's a homemade gift. I feel like I'm throwing away their love and hard work. Don't get me wrong, I love homemade gifts. It's just that I have come to allow myself to get rid of them after a while, which I used to think was unacceptable.

Yet, in order to prepare for my big dream of living in a tiny house, I was challenged to face the fact that if I didn't get rid of "stuff" then my tiny house would always be a big mess!

I have to remind myself that I *am* keeping other gifts from that same person. I only keep my favorites now.

Hoarding was My Love Language

But for one month, I decided to try a new idea that I'd heard.

Actually, the reason I tried it is because my sister said I could bring stuff to contribute to her yard sale. Then she put in the newspaper that she was having a 3-family yard sale and *I* was one of those families! So I figured I should bring a lot of stuff. I had a week to gather items. I took some stuff my mom was getting rid of, but it still wasn't much. I was working full-time, so I committed to **simply get rid of 10 items a day**. Bam! I'd have 50 by the end of the week.

At the yard sale, someone asked how much I wanted for the car buffer. My mom had had it in her pile to donate, and I didn't know what a car buffer was or if it even worked. When I said, "$3?" I could tell by the looks on their faces that it was a ridiculously low price. (I don't know what brand it was, but from what I can see from a quick Google search, they range from about $17-$160 new.) One of the gentlemen said, "Well, even if it doesn't work, it's worth that much just to try it." I loved it because it's still more money than we would've gotten otherwise. I didn't have to deal with it anymore, and it was obviously making their day.

That method brought such great results that I decided to continue for the rest of the month. Some nights after a long day at work, I would spend a mere 10 minutes getting rid of *more* than 10 things…partly due to the fact that it was boxes of stuff from college days, which made it easier to get rid of because it had nothing to do with my current lifestyle.

I consider it a success (even though I didn't stick with it completely) because I still got rid of about 100 items. Even though it showed me how much I enjoy the freedom of having less, I still had plenty I was emotionally attached to and had to deal with in a different way.

But what made this method of decluttering work for me?

I didn't have to spend grueling hours sorting through boxes of papers to see if I should keep each one or not. I didn't have to make a decision about *every* item. So much thinking! No, I just glanced around and said, "Hey, why do I still have this? It can count as one of my ten items." Or, "I won't use this for years, and it takes up lots of space. I bet someone will buy it, and then I can get another at a thrift store or online if I miss it." I only focused on the stuff that would be easy for me to get rid of.

However, after a month, I was tired of that method. I have gone back to it occasionally since then, but for the next month I decided to join a group of people getting rid of a bag of stuff a day. It seemed similar to what I was already doing, but my approach this time was to first list the areas of my house that needed the most attention. Then **I took a close-up "before" photo** of that area. Have you done that yet? Let me share a reminder and go a little more in-depth with why that was so helpful and important for me.

I've done plenty of decluttering before without taking pictures first. Taking a "before" picture works so well because it makes me want to see the "after" picture. That's some serious motivation.

When I tried taking a "before" picture in the past, it was of an entire room, which required me to declutter *an entire room* before I could see the difference. It helped to take pictures of one drawer, which I could declutter in about 20 minutes. Then I'd quickly be able to compare "before" and "after," which made me feel so accomplished. **The tiny act of taking a picture made a big difference.** It made me want to transform the rest of my room.

That feeling of accomplishment was caused by my brain's release of dopamine due to my small success. This is why we see people who make one positive change in their lives continue to improve in other areas, and people who struggle seem to continue to spiral downward until they make one positive change. Behaviorally, when we receive small rewards, we're more likely to repeat the action. It's part of how our brains function. None of that happened for me when taking a picture of an entire room, though.

It was also helpful for me to **join decluttering groups online** at that time because after I'd done all the hard work, I had something to show for it. The great part about pictures is that they're digital now, which means there's no extra cost. They only take up digital space and can easily be shared and then deleted with the click of a button. In these decluttering groups, I could share my "before" and "after" pictures with people who would be encouraging and understanding.

At the same time, I was able to motivate *them*.

I wouldn't invite tons of people inside my entire messy room just to see a tiny clean area, but I was okay with showing the part that I had cleaned (even though I also shared the messy picture). This accountability in decluttering is exciting because online communities among strangers haven't always been so common. I'm glad I get to take advantage of it! I continually get comments on what I've done, which encourages me to keep going with it.

Finding time to declutter is hard, so if it was going to happen, I had to make it a priority. (See the list at the end of this book for resources that helped keep my momentum going.) While I used to think hoarding gifts was a way of letting the gift-givers know that I love the time and effort they put into it, I now see how the hordes of clothing and pictures and figurines were adding to the chaos of my life and also the lives of the ones I love. They were taking on my clutter because my collections were spilling over into their space, and it was becoming a burden for them. That's no way to show love. If I really wanted to express my love and gratitude to those around me, something had to change. *I* had to change.

After participating in a yard sale, taking pictures of my clutter, and joining supportive groups so that my love languages no longer led to hoarding, it was time to work on a full-force plan. I had seen what a little decluttering could do and was ready to feel the freedom of even greater results.

Day 6

5-min Task

Post a Before picture of a small area you want to work on to a FB group, or text it to a friend. This will seriously motivate you to declutter so you can share the After picture!

Seven

IT MATTERS WHERE YOU START

"A good plan is like a road map: it shows the final
destination and usually the best way to get there."
-H. Stanley Judd

At eight years old, I had about fifty erasers of different shapes and colors, and I remember vividly how I arranged them into a whole little world with characters and stories. Back then, I thought organizing items was the way to make a room look nice. Plus, the process was fun and easy.

In sixth grade, we did a personality test where we circled one of four words that described us best. Being a packrat, I of course kept that paper. When I looked back at it years later, I realized the irony of me circling "indecisive" and then erasing it to circle another of the four words. I guess I was right the first time.

Unlike organizing, decluttering is full of *irreversible decisions*. Once you get rid of something, you can't get it back (especially when you're a kid with no income). Because I always wanted to make the right choice, getting rid of stuff was time-consuming and too much of a struggle. Maybe my little world would've looked better if I'd gotten rid of twenty of those erasers, but what if I would've missed one of them later?

As an adult, decision-making was already easier since I'd had more experience. Yet as I kept decluttering, I also kept getting even faster and better at making decisions. Since then, I've had hardly any moments of regret about what I've gotten rid of. I actually can't think of *any* examples. Having a decluttered life just makes such a difference that I know it's worth the possibility of regretting a few items I let go.

Because it was January when I started writing my decluttering plan, I had people encouraging me in setting goals for the new year. During that time, I kept hearing about a book called *The Life-Changing Magic of Tidying Up*. In it, the author recommends decluttering by *category* rather than *section* of the house in order to avoid moving the clutter around from room to room. Instead, each room gets a little less cluttered after going through each category. I was already in the habit of focusing on one personal goal a month, so I chose a different category for each month.

This simplified things because it made the plan easier to implement. **I didn't have to find and consult a list before each decluttering session because it was easy to remember on my own.**

I would, however, list out everything that I wanted to include in each category (ex: "Entertainment: Books, CDs, DVDs") so that I wouldn't accidentally overlook an item. Once I neared the end of the month, I'd check the list to see if there was anything left undone.

My Overall Decluttering Plan

I'm sharing my plan here as an example. Use it as a source of ideas. You may not have Christmas cards you need to go through, but maybe you have stationery you need to decide if you still want to use. Be specific and adjust the categories to your needs. Use the plan below as a starting point and add your own changes and ideas, especially changing the month to make it fit with the time of year when you're beginning.

Six Month Decluttering Plan

January: Clothes, shoes, bags, scarves, etc.

February: Books, CDs, DVDs

March: Dishes, appliances, food

April: Bills, receipts, newspapers, magazines, junk drawers, Christmas cards

May: Craft/hobby supplies, jewelry, toys, toiletries, cosmetics

June: Photos, memorabilia, tax info

While I grouped items together that were similar to me in some way, maybe you want jewelry to be in the category with clothing, especially if you have pieces that only go with certain outfits.

I've had people who began decluttering in June or July and aimed for being Clutter-Free by Thanksgiving, which is the title of the challenge I host in the Living Tiny Dreaming Big Facebook group each year, or Christmas or the New Year. That way, by the time they finished, they were able to celebrate with family and friends in a more peaceful environment. Plus, nothing ruins those family photos like a bunch of clutter in the background!

Another option is to set the goal as being clutter-free by a birthday or anniversary.

I love that the end of each month of this plan gave me an extra motivation to wrap up what I hadn't covered in that month's category. The beginning of the month renewed my excitement because I got to switch gears and start fresh in a new category. The first few days and the last few days worked as a trigger to remind me to keep decluttering in order to reach my goal on time.

If you want to know the reasons behind the order I chose to do these categories, check out the book *The Life-Changing Magic of Tidying Up*. Most of my reasons are there. But I wanted to mention that there are reasons for going in that order, in case simply knowing that helps you to follow it.

This quote by Douglas H. Everett captures what my decluttering plan helped me accomplish: "There are some people who live in a dream world, and there are some who face reality; and then there are those who turn one into the other." I lived in a dream world for so long by actually convincing myself that everything was great in relation to my clutter. Once I finally faced the reality that I was a packrat and didn't want to be, then I was able to start changing my reality into something better.

I used to think my story of becoming clutter-free had begun at the moment I made the decision to try to declutter. Or at least when I decided I wanted a tiny house.

But it really began when I was a child.
I had to look back at where my journey of becoming a packrat began so I could change the packrat mindset I'd unknowingly built and reinforced for years.

If I had never become a packrat, I would never have had to become clutter-free. I would've just always been that way. But my packrat ways manifested themselves in everything from my dislike of wasting anything to my indecisive nature. The process of changing was slow.

When I first started decluttering, I was picky about what I got rid of. If I had started off aggressively, the process may have turned out differently, with a sense of regret or loss, since I hadn't fully shifted my mindset. But for now, my only regret is that I didn't get rid of *more* to begin with so I could already be done with it and living with less clutter. Instead, I'm going through what I still have left all over again to see what else I can get rid of. And that's okay. I wouldn't have made it to this point without first taking those small steps.

Having a plan of *what* to declutter is what made those steps possible, but there was still a shift that needed to take place in the way I *thought* about both clutter *and* the process of getting rid of it. I needed time and proof to overcome the excuse that I was bad at decision-making. And once I did, I got better at it. I also had to stop using the excuse that I might regret getting rid of an item. And once I did, I got rid of tons of things without regret. But I still had more excuses!

Day 7
5-min Task
Search your house for the *largest* items you can get rid of. This builds your momentum because it give you a quick visual and taste of the freedom and other benefits being clutter-free will give you.

Eight

OVERCOMING EXCUSES

"It is better to offer no excuse than a bad one."
-George Washington

I once went to my friend's house, and she was wearing my clothes! I was about ten years old and was horrified. My mom had given away a bag of my clothes without me knowing. I still remember searching my room for my favorite shirt and not finding it. It was a black, long sleeves, collared button-up with bright blue, green, and purple checkered stripes. So stylish, I know. It was cuter than it sounds, okay?

My mother wouldn't have done that if she'd known how much it would bother me. But like so many of us, she didn't know how to get rid of stuff in a way that would minimize regret. She taught me many good skills, habits, and character qualities, but living a clutter-free life wasn't one of them. She did, however, raise me to have a *hunger* for a clutter-free life, partly because I saw how frustrating and inconvenient living a cluttered life could be.

I also kept learning about how to "reduce, reuse, and recycle" in school. I'm not against that. In fact, I guess my problem is that I was too *for* it. I never focused on how much I was letting the stuff I reused *waste space* by taking over. I felt so bad throwing things away only to have them end up in a landfill that my *house* became a landfill! I spent so much time and effort taking care of those unnecessary items instead of taking care of the space I had. I wasn't taught the value of open space except for the outdoors. Maybe that's part of what caused me to love being outside so much: there was always room to run and play and breathe and be creative.

I could go on about how my upbringing trained me to be a packrat (big family, low income, accepting almost anything free, placing value on family and friends in a way that promotes sentimental attachment and concern for the feelings of those who gave the gift, etc.), but **the important thing is that all of the mindsets that went along with how I was raised are *reversible*.** Merriam-Webster defines a mindset as a "mental attitude or inclination." I needed my natural inclination to change in order for me to be clutter-free, so I changed my mental attitude about clutter. And whatever attitudes you grew up with about possessions can also be changed.

It's not that I have to stop valuing family, but instead I can value them in a way that still allows me to be clutter-free. I'm also not saying that I don't ever accept free stuff, but now I'm more particular about which items I take. I make sure they're worth the trouble and that they really bring joy. And if I later find that they don't, then I get rid of them.

I can find a way around any excuse I have for keeping something. I just need the desire to look for one.

There are two things strong enough to give me the desire to overcome my excuses:

1) Seeing the benefits of decluttering: that it's worth it, it lines up with my values, and it propels me toward my goals in the long run rather than taking time away from them.

2) Knowing that decluttering isn't just organizing and that **what I'm doing is bringing permanent change**. When I declutter, I won't have to waste my time getting rid of the same items over and over. **Once I get an item out of the house, I don't have to deal with it ever again.** This is unlike organizing where I'm rearranging the same items over and over because things get disorganized again quickly, especially when there are lots of items and multiple people dealing with those items on a daily basis.

Something else that helped me overcome excuses was learning that they *can* be overcome…and by observing how other people have already overcome them.

Let me start with an example that has nothing to do with clutter.

I'm pretty sure I'm not the only one to ever have a good excuse for not turning in homework. Like a legitimately reasonable excuse of something beyond my control that happened.

Let's say a grandparent passed away for example.

But then there's always that Hermione in class who's like, "I had a stomach virus and was in a car wreck, but I still finished my homework."

And I'm just like, "What? *Why?!*"

But I think I'm starting to understand. The best thing I learned while decluttering was how to address my excuses. Once I realized I was making excuses, I was able to make changes if I didn't like what was going on in that area of my life.

If I'm looking for an excuse not to do something, believe me, I can find it. Queen of Excuses right here. Excuses aren't just for convincing other people. They are the way I talk myself into believing I'm right in the choices I make.

When I'm determined to do one thing (declutter) and something else comes up (car trouble), my question *now* is, "How can I deal with this car *and* still accomplish the decluttering task I'm determined to complete?" When I approach it this way instead of just saying, "Great. Now I have to do this other thing, so I can't declutter," then a solution usually comes to mind. Maybe I cut out something less important. Maybe instead of decluttering for thirty minutes, I do only fifteen minutes of decluttering. It's much easier to stay focused and work quickly for fifteen minutes than for thirty.

When I ignore the unexpected problems that come up and act like they're not a big deal, things get worse. But it's so much better when I say, "Yes, I have a good excuse (or three) for not decluttering, but how can I do it anyway even on a small level?" That way, interruptions don't defeat me; they only slow me down.

Good Excuses VS. Bad Excuses

In relation to a goal, a bad excuse is one that keeps me from reaching that goal or establishing a habit I want to develop. A *good* excuse is simply one that helps me reach my goals. It lines up with my beliefs.

In order to turn a bad excuse into a good one, I need to know my values. For me, health is very important, but I never associated being clutter-free with being healthier. Once I did, I was able to see that my excuses were hurting me rather than helping.

For years I considered myself to be adequately healthy:

- I had great relationships
- I drank water almost exclusively
- I stayed active
- I journaled
- I even paid off $25k of student loans in three years

But for all those years, I lived with clutter. I thought it was a "sacrifice" I had to make if I was going to continue succeeding in other areas of my life.

Decluttering seemed like an unhealthy waste of time and energy. Sure, I liked for things to be clutter-free, but it wasn't worth the effort. It really just didn't seem practical for me.

I made every excuse I could. But once I changed my mindset and realized my excuses weren't as great as I thought, I decided to make excuses *to* declutter instead of not to.

I still have some decluttering to do, but I'm also not defeated by it anymore even though it seems never-ending. I know it's actually a process that takes time. While it doesn't happen overnight, I'll eventually have an amount of items I'm happy with. Then it won't require so much effort to manage it.

For now, here are the decluttering excuses I still use, which took me almost a year to learn.

Old excuse: I don't have time to declutter.

New excuse: I don't have time for extra hours at work right now. Decluttering is a better use of my time, at least until I've gone through every category once.

That's the process behind the first step of defeating clutter: I decided to take my excuse for not decluttering and then overcome it by making a new excuse stating why or how I would declutter anyway. Here's another example:

Old excuse: I don't want to declutter. It's too hard, and in a few months it'll end up looking the same as before.

New excuse: I want the results that come with being clutter-free. I'm willing to invest my time and effort into making decluttering a priority in order to improve my life and the lives of others. I'll develop a system that works for me to keep the clutter away. It's harder to live with clutter than to get rid of it.

I've been *slowly* decluttering over the last few years (and quickly decluttering for part of that time). But I had to change nearly every mindset I had about clutter before I started to see a noticeable difference in the amount of stuff I have.

It was a game-changer for me to *believe I could* declutter and maintain a clutter-free lifestyle as well as good relationships. I thought decluttering would take away from my relationships because I'd have less time for them, but it really was quite the opposite.

It was important to see that decluttering would benefit my dreams of traveling and writing instead of seeing it as a nuisance taking me away from what I love.

I've since learned that traveling is so much easier and more fun when I'm not carrying extra weight! I learned from my decluttering adventures how to pack light.

As for writing, my first book is about decluttering. It gave me something to write about and a way to help other people, so it's definitely making that dream a reality.

Getting rid of clutter taught me self-discipline, which has assisted me in every other area of life. It taught me to say no to things that aren't so important to me, like free clothes that aren't my style, and to say yes to what matters, like writing a book. I had to see that getting rid of clutter was just another way of adding to my overall health.

The first several months of eliminating clutter had already given me freedom and hope. And it started with that one step of changing my mindset.

Instead of holding onto my excuses, I had to make myself see the benefits of a clutter-free life.

An Incomplete List of the Benefits of Being Clutter-Free:

Thinking more clearly. When my space is clean, my mind is clear, which benefits all other areas of my health.

Good eating habits. It's easier to eat better when I'm less stressed. And for me, less clutter in my room and schedule equals less stress.

Contentment. Even though I was happy before, it was in spite of the clutter. Just beginning to become clutter-free has added to my satisfaction with life. At the same time, it has made me more hopeful about the future.

Motivation. With less clutter, there's more room to be creative. There's more time and space to pursue goals. I also have more energy to put into those goals and hobbies.

Self-Care. I didn't expect getting rid of clutter to change my appearance. I used to think make-up and fashion were a waste of time and money. Now though, I actually have time to learn quick, inexpensive tricks for improving my outward appearance while still having time to improving who I am and how I help others. I no longer see them as mutually exclusive. I've come to realize I enjoy getting dolled up a couple of times a week. Because I'm spending less time taking care of excess items, I have more time to take care of myself. Self-care products also don't get lost in all the clutter. Since I only keep items that make a noticeable difference, I get excited about using them. They were worth keeping even after three rounds of decluttering.

It's a Lifestyle

Becoming clutter-free is no small matter for me. I still shock myself by things I say and do, things I've never done or even *thought* before.

It's a huge lifestyle change for a packrat.

It wasn't an intense three-day task like I thought it would be. I've had to take it slowly, incorporating it into my daily life. I couldn't put the rest of my life on hold until I finished. It takes too long for that; I would've given up.

Similar to losing weight or getting out of debt, I had to be in it for the long haul or clutter would sneak back in with my bad habits and old excuses. In fact, with my clothing, it kind of already has. I had my wardrobe looking and feeling great. But over the year since I began it, I have added extra items without removing as many. Part of that is due to the nature of changing jobs and lifestyles, but it's time for me to go through it again. Yet I'm even more excited this time because I've already experienced the benefits, and I know it won't take as much time and effort as before.

That's why I don't want someone to declutter *for* me. I need to develop the discipline and habit of telling myself no, of letting go of what holds me back. That's exactly what I did, and I'll share that process throughout the rest of the book. But I'm going to start by sharing how I dealt with feeling like I don't have time to declutter.

Day 8
5-min Task
Find 10 items to get rid of. Add them to your Donation Station.

Nine

WHAT IF I DON'T HAVE TIME?

"I just don't have the time" often means
"I just don't have the self-discipline."
-Winifred Gallagher,

Rapt: Attention & the Focused Life

When I moved out of my college apartment, I had a couple of guys help me load stuff into vehicles. I was trying to make some last-minute decisions on what to get rid of, but they were in a hurry to get it all taken care of.

"Just pack it all and go through it later," they said.

And that's what I did.

You wanna guess how much later it was before I went through it all?

Four years.

Years!

I don't want that to be me again.

Before I learned what decluttering was and how to do it, I thought, "I just don't have time for that."

But I decided I'd *make* the time and not allow myself to be rushed.

The first thing I let go of was one of my jobs. I know this isn't practical for everyone, but doing that helped me eliminate some of my excuses for not decluttering. I also didn't have to permanently give up that extra work. But there are still ways to declutter even while working a full-time job, which is part of why I've included this chapter.

I was a college student, a world traveler, then a full-time nanny—which meant I was basically a mother of four. Or I was away at a job where I only brought a car full of necessities with me anyway, so all my clutter was hours away.

Our time is valuable. So I want to share the quickest and biggest changes I implemented over years of studying simplicity.

These changes don't happen over a weekend, but they can make a big difference in a relatively short amount of time. A month of doing the following made a big enough difference that it kept me motivated to continue and even see an end in sight.

How I Save Time Decluttering

First, **I make getting rid of stuff simple.** If figuring out where and how to sell an item keeps me from getting rid of it, I just give it away. That's usually more fun. Plus, it's faster. The only items I've consistently sold are books because I have three great used bookstores nearby. It's fast, convenient, and fun.

Then I ask just one question about each item. For the most part, I don't ask, "Do I use this? Will I ever use it? Should I keep it in case someone else needs it someday? Should I keep it since I paid a lot for it? Should I keep it since my friend gave it to me?" etc. Instead, I use the KonMari method and ask if it's something I'm excited about keeping. If it isn't *adding* joy, then it is *taking* joy from my life. That makes it easier to part with. But sometimes it can be tricky because, with certain items, one aspect of it makes me excited to keep it while another function of it steals joy. That's when I use the questions listed in the chapter titled "From Frustration to Freedom." That way I'm not necessarily keeping those items just because they make me happy in a small way.

I was so glad I put in the time and effort when I did so that I could focus on more important things later—instead of repeating the same time-consuming routines.

If you really "don't have time," there are still a few options.

1) Rearrange your schedule so you *do* have time.

- This may mean delegating other tasks you normally do, such as cleaning or cooking, in order to temporarily put that time and effort into decluttering.

- Or maybe it means saying no—even to something good, like volunteer work—for six months.

- Be sure to write it down! If you make a list of what you want to accomplish each day, write "declutter" on that list. If you live by your calendar, add it there just like you do for other important appointments you don't want to miss.

2) Incorporate decluttering into something you already do, such as spending time with a friend or family member.

3) It could even be helpful to hire help, but the guidelines later in this chapter need to be followed or it could end up causing more work with little results and taking up more time than it's worth.

Getting the Right Help

Since I have a blog that deals a lot with getting rid of clutter, I have many people ask how to get other people to do the same (usually people they live with). And because I never thought I'd declutter, I want to help more people who are like I was realize that decluttering is not only possible but also very fulfilling. Since I've been where they are, I know a way that I can really improve their lives.

So I wrote a post on my blog similar to what I'm about to share here. It's probably the post I've gotten the most tremendous feedback on. **I received comments from both those who were trying to help others declutter and those who were trying to get someone to help them declutter.**

Just because someone knows how to be clutter-free, doesn't mean they know how to teach someone else.

Because people have different views on what's valuable, I couldn't have someone do the work of decluttering for me even if I could afford it. They'd get rid of things I loved and keep things I hate. Likewise, when I was helping my mom, I couldn't get rid of her stuff for her. I could help her decide what to get rid of. I could carry boxes and ask questions. But she had to be there, too, making decisions about what to let go of.

I've often witnessed someone "help" another person declutter. You know, when the person tells you everything you should keep and get rid of? Whether it's a family member, friend, or hired professional, it can be stressful. I know it was for me.

This section is a result of all the bad experiences I've had with someone helping me declutter. I hope to help others avoid that trouble but also realize they don't have to declutter alone to get stuff done *and* be able to keep what they want.

Packrats can be really embarrassed to have other people see all the clutter that they don't even remember having. Sometimes a helper makes me feel even worse about all my possessions. They have good intentions, so I try to be sure to let them know how grateful I am for their help. But before we tackle clutter together, we both need to know what's helpful and what's not.

When I help my clients, I advise them to read the information in this chapter and have whoever helps them do the same so they're both on the same page. If there are parts the person who is decluttering doesn't agree with, I recommend them letting their helper know that ahead of time so they can both get the most done in the time they set aside.

Guidelines for Helping Others Declutter

What *Isn't* Helpful

> • *Being condescending.* Asking questions like, "Eww, why did you keep this?" doesn't really make me want to continue decluttering. It makes me associate getting rid of stuff with even more negativity because I feel stupid and guilty. However, there's a huge difference if *I* were to say

something similar, like: "I don't know why I even kept this." It's just like when someone doesn't want anyone to talk bad about their family, but when *they* bring it up, it's okay. The same is true if *I'm* the one who makes fun of my clutter. It can be a nice, lighthearted moment. But when my helper brings it up, it puts a damper on the situation.

• *Asking questions that make the declutterer think about why they want to keep the item.* If my helper asks, "When are you gonna use it?" then I, being the creative genius that I am, come up with a scenario of when I might actually have a use for it. And implying that my stuff is a piece of junk that no one else would want, just makes me want to keep it even more. It reminds me that there's probably no one else who would take care of it and give it a home. Even if my helper has struggled with clutter, they may not know my reasons for accumulation. It helps to keep in mind that what works for one person might not work for the other.

• *Telling them they need to "just get it cleaned up."* Most likely, I've already told myself the same thing and come up with lots of excuses not to get it cleaned up anyway. And yet I'm obviously finally making the effort to do something about it. The last thing I want to hear is I need to rush or am not doing enough.

Instead, the helper can encourage the declutterer by doing some of the following…

What *is* Helpful

• *Let the declutterer make the decision about what to keep and what not to keep.* A big reason people don't get rid of stuff is because they're afraid they'll regret it later. If I'm pressured into parting with something, I'm usually upset about it later.

• *Ask questions to help the declutterer figure out if an item is something they want to keep.* I frequently help clients decide what to do with something by asking them questions from chapter eight. But I'm sure I have kept items of my own that they'd be perfectly willing to toss because we are different and have different priorities. It's easy for people to get rid of someone else's stuff because they don't care about it or use it like the owner of that item does.

• *Keep it fun!* I don't like being rushed, but I love when someone makes it a competition to see how many bags we can fill. It also helps to plan short breaks with motivating rewards.

• *Offer to take the items they don't want when you go.* I'd say this is the most helpful thing of all! If the helper can drop the donation pile off at a center, it helps the declutterer see immediate results more clearly and stay motivated even after the helper is gone.

Once I think these things through, they make perfect sense. But sometimes we don't take the time to focus on what we're saying or doing.

This message really resonated with my readers. In fact, one of them mentioned that she had seen both strategies in one household. She had helped some people declutter using the strategies I described above as helpful. They ended up decluttering three rooms. The children of the people she helped practiced all the things I listed that you *shouldn't* do, and the result was tears and arguments.

When done the wrong way, decluttering can damage relationships, but when done well, it can enhance them. And that's the best reason for decluttering.

When I feel bad staying home to declutter instead of running errands or working extra hours to relieve some of the burden from my family, I remind myself that making the time to get rid of clutter is another way for me to ease the burdens of the ones I love. I was able to give back space in their homes. **I'm so grateful I didn't drag nearly as much stuff into my marriage as I would've if I had gotten married just three years earlier.** But none of that would have happened if I hadn't made the process fun!

Day 9

5-min Task

Rate the state of your clutter on a scale of 1-10, with 10 being the worst. Add it to your progress tracking paper. Every few months, you can rate it again to measure whether or not you're headed in the direction you want to go.

Ten

ESTABLISHING FUN HABITS

"People rarely succeed unless they have fun
in what they are doing."
- Dale Carnegie

I decided that since I'd be spending so much time decluttering, I would make it fun.

When I'm busy doing something else that I view as important, cleaning and decluttering can quickly become what seems like a necessary evil.

But when I instead think of how having a clutter-free space can benefit me in other areas of life, I don't feel guilty about making time for it. And once I have time for decluttering, I can actually have fun with it!

Decluttering used to seem about as much fun as following a list of rules against all the things I like doing. So I wanted to make a new list.

M. C. Starbuck

{ This one's for the rule-breakers. }

Clutter Rules!

Rule 1: Throw everything out the window!

Rule 2: Buy things just because they're on sale.

Rule 3: Put anything you don't have a place for in piles on the floor. Keep adding to the piles.

Rule 4: Fit as much stuff as you can into one room so you can close the door when company is over. After they leave, take hours to find stuff when you need it!

Rule 5: Don't bother encouraging others to declutter.

Rule 6: Whatever you do, don't read stories about how people downsized.

Rule 7: Don't watch *Hoarders*. I know you want to, but resist the urge. I believe in you!

Rule 8: Don't get rid of *anything,* even if it would only take five minutes.

Rule 9: Don't be grateful for what you already have. Always be on the lookout for something new!

Rule 10: Accept anything that's free. It's free! Hello! Take it home and fill your house with free stuff until you have to buy a bigger house because you have so much awesome free stuff. That isn't a hassle at all.

Rule 11: Remember, you might use it one day. It's not like you could go to a thrift store or dollar store or online and get it if you actually want to use it. No, you need to keep it now in a pile that makes you cringe to go near it because it screams obligation.

Sometimes a bit of fun reverse psychology is all I need to help conquer more of my clutter.

Now back to some non-reverse psychology...

Even while I was a packrat, if I *knew* I'd get a million dollars for spending thirty minutes a day getting rid of stuff for 250 days out of the year, you know I would've done it, right?

I mean, *I would've made it happen*. Not that I'm all about money, but you can do a lot of good in the world with a million dollars.

I'd have set aside other projects until I'd finished this one. I'd have rearranged my life a little. I'd have told people "no" so I could focus on decluttering, even though I wasn't fond of it.

I still wouldn't have to say "no" to everything. It's only 30 minutes. But you better believe I wouldn't be making excuses to get out of that 30 minutes.

And I'd be cautious about skipping days, especially at the beginning, because I'd want to make sure I get all 250 days in. I'd only pause my progress for death-in-the-family or once-in-a-lifetime type situations. Then I could take a vacation later. I'd still have over 100 days that year where I wouldn't have to declutter.

I would've made it a priority because I'd see how it could help me reach other goals after a short time. I would've been able to pay for more travel, pay off student loans, and pay cash for a house on a beautiful acreage.

Yet if someone had challenged me to do that without the offer of a million dollars, I would've been much more lax about it. I probably wouldn't even have tried at all.

I needed a big incentive to start decluttering.

It's obvious that I'm not the only one with that view or everyone would be clutter-free. A huge part of the problem is that we don't see the *value* of getting rid of clutter.

I'm not giving you a million dollars, but I honestly believe that what we gain from decluttering is worth even more than that.

Changing My Mind

Let's face it, we could have a million bucks and still be stressed. We might be able to afford a bigger house, but without changing our habits, that big house could become just as cluttered as our current home.

There's a shift that has to take place in the way we think about clutter, as well as the process of getting rid of it. This is different than just the excuses I shared earlier. It's about our entire *mindset*.

After decluttering for about six months, though, I had developed a mindset that helped me establish habits and overcome obstacles in other areas of my life.

The *packrat mindset* is that decluttering is a poor use of time. Aren't there so many better things I could be doing? Things that are more meaningful and fun?

But the *clutter-free mindset* is that decluttering helps every other area of my life: relationships, mental health, physical health, spiritual health, and finances.

A precious lady in her 70s that I know from my mom's church told me recently that she used to go shopping when she was mad. Now she declutters! She doesn't do it every time, but I still love how she's using decluttering for her benefit. She said shopping helps get her mind off whatever's bothering her; whereas, decluttering is a physical activity that releases her pent up emotions. Decluttering is helping her use her negative energy in a positive way instead of using it in a way she'll regret later, like when she has less money for what she really wants or when she has piles of new stuff in her way.

Plenty of people don't think working out is fun. I'm one of them. But I can see the benefit of it, so I know that the effort is worth it. So sometimes I do work out in the traditional sense. But I also try to make being active a part of my lifestyle as well as something fun.

For example, I frequently work outdoors, taking students on hikes. I get paid to exercise. Or I go swimming. It doesn't feel like a workout because it's fun, but I'm getting those same benefits.

That's what I did with decluttering. It isn't very fun when I don't see progress or when my decluttering isn't effective. It was key, therefore, to make a lasting and noticeable difference, especially early in the decluttering process.

Sometimes it felt very much like work. But other times it was a stress-reliever. Sometimes I was decluttering alone. Other times it was almost a family competition to see who could get rid of the most.

Good Rewards for Good Behaviors

Rewarding ourselves for hard work or winning a competition is important. But it's also important to make the reward something that encourages our habit rather than destroys it. So for decluttering, we probably *shouldn't* give ourselves a reward like this after decluttering for 30 days: Take a break from decluttering for a week and spend $30 at yard sales.

Gretchen Rubin is an expert on habits and happiness. On her podcast, she explains what would and wouldn't be a good reward. Taking a break wouldn't be a good reward because it makes decluttering seem like a negative task that we need a break from. And it gets us out of the routine and momentum of doing it.

That's not to say that there won't naturally be weeks where less decluttering gets done, but let's not schedule an extra one in there just for fun.

As Rubin also explains, a better reward would be one that encourages our habit. I like rewards that make decluttering easier or more fun.

For example, my reward could be that I invite people over. It's fun, but it also will motivate me to do more last-minute decluttering. Or my reward could be that I hire someone to haul some stuff off for me after I've decluttered for a certain amount of time. In addition to making me want to get rid of more before help arrives to take it away, this reward also makes the process of decluttering easier on me.

My sister and one of her friends paid to have a large dumpster placed in their yard for a week. They were able to fill it and have it all taken away quickly with minimal extra work for them. That was a good reward for them because they have big families, so it really helped. It wasn't the best option for me since I lived with other people.

How I Made It Fun

So, how did I make rewards fun for me? Stickers, of course! For every time I filled a bin and donated the contents, I put a sticker on it. (I've also kept a piece of paper by my donation boxes and simply add the stickers there.) Not only was it fun, but it helped me see how much I'd gotten out of my house. No wonder I could breathe easier.

Sometimes I'd think I hadn't gotten rid of much since my room was still crowded. Then I'd look at those stickers and be so glad I didn't still have all the stuff they represent.

I stopped this practice after the first six months of decluttering. I switched to a smaller, prettier container to hold what I'm getting rid of. Since I'd gotten rid of most of my clutter, I no longer needed a huge container. I wanted to replace the large one with a cute container as a reward for my diligence. Having a container that wasn't as unseemly renewed my excitement about the way my home looked and about the decluttering process.

Other little things like that can make it fun, too, but really the process itself just became enjoyable because I was finding things I'd been looking for and gaining freedom from things I used to think I should keep. It became more of a game and competition with myself to see if I could find even more to get rid of.

When it actually makes a difference in how things look and feel, it's just more fun. It's refreshing to open a drawer or door and be able to see everything inside. It's exciting to be able to find an item I need and then have a place to return it.

When we don't know how to overcome the excuses that keep us from getting started and how to use them to our advantage, then we'll never have the chance to experience all the fun decluttering can be.

And sometimes there have been rewards and fun moments while decluttering that I didn't plan or even anticipate. I get super excited about some of the cute little things I find!

One week I could *not believe* I found a $100 bill in a recipe box I don't even use! I'm not the type to hide money from myself so I don't spend it, but about 10 days later I found the envelopes I had used for Dave Ramsey's envelope system for a while. I opened the first one. Empty. I opened the second one to find $140! There were about ten envelopes, and it was *so fun* opening each one and finding more cash. I felt so rich. I figured the total was about $250, but when I added it all up, it was $403, bringing my total to over $500 found that week while decluttering. *That's* fun! That was over two weeks of income for me!

Even with help and rewards, decluttering can be frustrating. But thankfully, I experienced enough positive outcomes to make the small amount of frustration completely worth it. Through decluttering, I was able to turn my frustration into freedom.

Day 10
5-min Task
Choose one simple way to make decluttering fun. Maybe wear a hat or some lipstick while you collect items for your Donation Station.

Eleven

FROM FRUSTRATION TO FREEDOM

"Maybe the life you've always wanted to live is buried
underneath everything you own."
-Joshua Becker

Frustrating. Sad. Meaningless. Drudgery.

These are things I used to associate with decluttering.

But these are words I associate with it now:
Freedom. Joy. Purpose. Fun.

Going from packrat to clutter-free was a fairly slow process to begin
with, but eventually my creativity was able to flourish. What made
it faster was changing my mindset. I did that by asking myself
specific questions that gave me clarity about what to do with each
item.

I'd heard people talk about not letting your possessions "own you." I honestly didn't think mine did. Once I answered the following questions about the items I was surrounded with every day, I realized how much control my stuff truly had over my daily life.

Clarifying Questions

1. Does it make me feel imprisoned?

Maybe it had bad memories associated with it. Maybe I felt obligated to keep it because it was a gift or because someone told me I should have one. I finally started to recognize that I could actually get rid of those items without regret and let those invisible chains fall away.

2. Could I buy it (or something similar or better) later?

I hadn't even thought about how easy online shopping and thrift stores have made it for me to buy items fairly quickly and inexpensively. Instead, I kept piles of things I wasn't even using. Asking this question helped me get rid of items without the fear that it would be super difficult to replace it if necessary.

3. Would I be happier without it?

I had some items I used only because they were there. That's why I sometimes don't agree with the advice of getting rid of items I haven't used. There are times when I don't use my favorite items simply because I can't find them in the midst of all the items I only kind of like.

For example, I had numerous outfits that looked so cute on the hanger, but not once I put them on. I would wear them because they were clean or convenient, but I didn't really like how they looked or felt while I was wearing them. I'm much happier without them because there's more room for my favorites.

4. What else could I do with the space?

I was so sentimental about the past that I was running out of space for new things. I didn't take time to think about how the memories I was currently making could be better if I had more space. I tell people all the time now: Dream about how you'd live differently if you had more space and less stuff. How would your holidays be less stressful? How would your daily life be improved so your everyday memories are better? I wish I'd asked myself those questions earlier in life.

I needed to be a little more sentimental about the future instead of just the past.

---

5. Could it benefit someone else more?

One of the most common questions people ask themselves is "What if I need it one day?" This led me to keep things I didn't need, just in case. I probably wouldn't be able to find that item even if I *did* need it.

Asking "Who might need this *now*?" has helped me find a place for the item to do what it was made for rather than take up space in my house.

6. Is it worth the trouble of keeping it?

It seems so much easier to keep an item when, to get rid of it, I have to first figure out who to give it to, load it into the car, and drive to drop it off, possibly in a different town.

But that's just because I'd forget the trouble the item causes me: how many times I've had to move it to open a drawer, or how annoyed I felt by remembering I needed to repair it, or what a pain it is to wash. If I could do without it, I made the effort to get rid of it so I no longer had the chores associated with taking care of it.

7. Would I buy this now if I saw it in a store?

Some of the things I have in my house would never catch my eye while out shopping. Yet I keep them in my house as if they were one of the best things in the world.

8. Does seeing it or thinking about it bring me joy?

When I'm surrounded by things that bring me joy, it follows that I become more joyful. And when I'm more joyful, that joy spreads to the people I love.

How These Questions Helped

Every time I glanced at it, the box of papers I needed to go through was taunting me. Once I faced it little by little, I was able to get rid of it *and* the frustration I got every time I saw it.

I didn't *have* to ask myself all these thought-provoking questions about each item, but they are worth asking.

These eight questions helped me notice how much space in my house and my mind was being taken up by things I didn't like or use. For so long, I just kept things by default. These items were robbing me of time I could have spent planning the vacation I ended up not taking because I ran out of time to adequately prepare.

I had allowed my possessions to take up space I could have used to help friends and family feel welcome and relaxed.

Using these questions has helped me get rid of more than:

- Thirty-one pounds of paper
- One hundred and twenty books
- Thirteen boxes of clothes and random stuff

If someone had told me a few years ago that I'd get rid of that much stuff, I would have been horrified. I would have said that I love my books too much to get rid of them. I mean, I spent four years getting an English degree! Yet I was able to easily let these items go without regret since my mindset had changed. I still enjoy reading, and I've probably read more than I used to because I have more time and focus now that I've gotten rid of so much excess.

Beauty & Freedom

Another benefit of asking myself these questions was that I was the one in charge of making each decision. No one else was telling me what my answers should be or that I should get rid of something. They weren't telling me I was stupid for having it in the first place.

It was actually a pleasant experience, and I've been able to see spaces in my room slowly open up.

These questions helped me get rid of items and uncover the life I'm living now so I can experience more of the beauty and freedom that comes from not letting my possessions own me.

Answered Prayers Have Their Downside

What's something you've really wanted? You may have prayed for a child, a spouse, or a job. Once you received it, though, you found yourself complaining about the sleepless nights or the lack of time for yourself. This is such a common occurrence that I wanted to address it before we go any further.

Right now, you want to be clutter-free, but there will come a day when you realize that being a packrat had its benefits, too. A friend of mine shared that when she helps people lose weight, they reach their goal and then realize they are getting more attention than they used to. That may sound nice in theory, but it can really bother you if you aren't used to it or ready for it. When those days come, you get to choose to see your progress as a blessing you've received rather than wanting to return to not caring how much stuff you accumulate.

Day 11

5-min Task

Gather all your jeans or all your leggings or all your skirts. Ask yourself of each item if you'd buy it again if you saw it in a store. If not, add it to your Donation Station.

Twelve

FROM PACKRAT TO CLUTTER-FREE

"A year from now,
you will wish you had started today."
-Karen Lamb

Imagine that in a year you could say you're no longer a packrat.

It's a crazy feeling.

This time a few years ago, I was still trying to organize my clutter while hardly getting rid of anything. One area would look great, but it wouldn't last.

When I focused instead on getting stuff out of my life, that's when real and permanent change began to happen.

I didn't just start decluttering because I suddenly realized it was a good idea.

There was something bigger that I wanted which required decluttering in order to get there.

And it wasn't just a tiny house.

I wanted space for creative work. (I seriously used to go outside or in my mom's living room to focus on reading or writing or to have room to exercise or work on a project.) I wanted freedom and simplicity.

In the previous chapter, I listed questions to ask about items while decluttering. But here are a few questions that were helpful for me to ask myself before I started following my decluttering plan.

The questions below have, at various stages in the process, helped me to be more diligent in getting rid of stuff because they remind me that I really want my future to be better than my past and even than the present.

It helps to ask:

What will I be doing a year from now?

If I were already clutter-free, how would I be able to spend this year differently?

What do I want that decluttering will help me get?

Some possible answers to that last question are:

More rest because I wouldn't frequently be moving clutter around as I need space in a certain area.

Better rest because I wouldn't keep seeing things that need to be done around the house. I'm able to relax and be creative instead.

Community because, without so much clutter, I won't be embarrassed to have people over. I can celebrate special occasions in the peacefulness of my own home if I'd like.

These are the kinds of things we need to keep telling ourselves until we're clutter-free. Maybe that means you write them on sticky notes and post them inside a cabinet you open frequently or on a notebook you use a lot or in your car. Or you could create a simple image and make it the background of your phone.

Focusing on the goal of being able to have people over is very important to me because I'm such a homebody, but I also enjoy making more than surface-level connections with others. I enjoy tea parties and discussing books and playing board games.

At my house growing up, this didn't happen much. I spent plenty of time with friends, but it was mostly at *their* houses.

We used to take pictures in front of the door. Why? Because that's the area we kept clutter-free because we had to use it to get in and out of the house or from room to room. Sometimes we would take a really good picture, but the background was such a mess that my mom didn't want anyone else to see it.

I don't want to face these same problems in my own home.

A lot of bad habits didn't seem like bad habits to me because they were just normal. It's no wonder it took me a year to reverse them. It's more surprising that it didn't take longer.

But what *did* take longer was actually getting rid of every bit of clutter. And that's okay. **I wouldn't expect someone who had been accumulating debt for 25 years to be able to pay it all off in one year, even if they had changed their mindsets and made some big lifestyle changes.**

69

Remembering this makes me even more enthusiastic about my efforts to get rid of stuff so I'm able to enjoy being without clutter for an even longer amount of time. **It shows me that I'm not behind in my work, and that I can even get rid of clutter in less time than I accumulated it**, if I'm intentional and diligent.

Being Selective

Lisa Byrne of The Art of Simple wrote, "When we become skilled at selectively knowing what to prune out of our lives, what remains becomes stronger, brighter, clearer." This reminds me how and why I should be intentional about getting rid of possessions.

My family has a peach tree in our yard, and we were so excited about all the fruit growing on it. The branches were so full of peaches that they broke under the weight, taking us from having an abundance of fruit to practically none. All because we didn't prune the tree.

The shelves and boxes in my house were in a similar condition, bending under the weight of my possessions. So many items remained useless because there was no way I could use them all or find them when I needed them. After "pruning" my house, I can breathe easier and function better because my burden is lighter.

It's so refreshing to be able to see my favorite clothes and books and memorabilia more often now that I've gotten rid of my least favorites. I know where so much more of my stuff is! It no longer gets lost in hard-to-reach places under a bed or forgotten about in boxes.

Returning to our tree the next year, my brother got rid of about half the peaches before they were even close to full size. That's where I am with my clutter now. It isn't overtaking me, so I'm able to manage it. Even though it's still work, it's much more productive than continuing to let everything pile up.

Even after I changed my mindsets and became more selective, I still had bad days of wanting to give up or complain that it's taking too long. Sometimes I still didn't think it was fun or feel like I had enough time. I've felt hopeless that the clutter would never end. A huge part of what helped me continue on those bad days was that I created an environment where a lot of people were counting on me. So let me explain how I did that without putting *too much* pressure on myself.

Day 12

5-min Task

Gather all your dressy shirts or dresses. When you come to an item you're on the fence about keeping, ask yourself: "Could I buy it again—or something similar or better—later?" If the answer is yes, get rid of it.

Thirteen

ACCOUNTABILITY

{ PEOPLE COUNTING ON ME }

"The right thing to do and the hard thing to do are
usually the same."
-Steve Maraboli

When I think of accountability, I often think of having someone who
follows up with me to make sure I'm doing what I've told them my
goal was. This method was only one aspect of the accountability that
worked for me. The problem with this method is that it leaves the
other person in charge. The excuse can then come up that they didn't
check in with me, so I forgot to do it.

What worked for me even more, was telling multiple people my
goals and deadlines. This did two things: made me set specific
deadlines for myself and put my integrity on the line. With more
people knowing about my plan, it was more likely that someone
would remember eventually. Even if they *didn't* remember the goals
and deadlines I'd chosen, I didn't want to be the person who went

back on her word. If I never make the promise public, I don't feel the importance of keeping it as strongly as when I do share it.

How I Unintentionally Created Accountability

I already had a blog about simplifying life when I started decluttering. It was fairly easy to turn that into a way to share my experience with clutter. I didn't wait until I was finished to share it with people. Instead, I almost immediately began encouraging others to simplify their lives, too.

They started expecting to hear from me about my progress and ideas that helped me. They became accustomed to me checking in on Facebook and giving them the chance to share their own accomplishments as well.

I started 30-Day Challenges that forced me to come up with ideas for decluttering every day. I offered 100 of my readers a copy of *The Life-Changing Magic of Tidying Up* (or a copy of *Do the Work* to those who already had the other), and received this amazing reply:

Hi, Megan!

I feel like I know you after being coached by you for 22 days. Your offer of the book is so generous! My husband actually bought the "tidying up" book (for himself) but I felt overwhelmed when I started to read it. I couldn't imagine going through everything at once--emptying out an entire closet for example...

But after being in this challenge and getting the encouragement you have offered, as well as the specific steps (although I haven't been 100% in compliance!), I can probably go back and read the book with a fresh perspective and receive encouragement from it instead of increased stress. Going from zero-to-60 was overwhelming, so your approach of 5 minutes a day was a welcome way to start.

There was another challenge that I had joined earlier in 2015 that was intended, I discovered after I joined, for people who stayed home all day and had nothing else to do but declutter. At least it seemed so because one day's task was "empty out all your kitchen cupboards, sort everything and toss half of it, and then put the other half back." One day! Oy!

Last weekend my husband and I donated 8 kitchen trash bags of clothing! It felt so good to get it out of our storage and into use again. I want to tackle my kitchen storage/Tupperware stash next!

So, thank you for the challenge, thank you for your spirit of compassion and encouragement, thank you for your exuberance that isn't irritating. Hehe...

I appreciate the offer of the second book, but I will look it up and order it for myself. I want someone else to be blessed by your generosity because I've already been blessed by you!

-S.W.

Wow! How's that for motivation to keep going?

Hearing about other people's progress, and seeing the impact that my journey was having on them, played a big role in helping me not give up. Even though I was one of those people who had nothing to do but declutter all day for a while, I still usually did other stuff, too.

I'd read, spend time with my family, and enjoy hobbies like painting.

I love that my experience of having to break big goals into small ones was beneficial for my readers. Now, some people could probably declutter their kitchen in a day because they have a lot less in their kitchen to begin with. Those challenges are valid and helpful. It just depends on the stage of life of the person. Some people probably saw my challenge and thought, "Why would I only spend five minutes decluttering? I wanna get stuff done!" Yet I knew there were already other challenges out there for people like that. I wanted to continue helping my readers who felt like me, like other stuff wasn't working for them. I wanted to show them they didn't have to give up, that there are others like them who make it work. I wanted to continue helping more people improve their lives and the lives of those around them.

Another one of my favorite emails helped me realize I was achieving that goal. It came from Phyllis a couple of years ago:

Dear Megan,

I have followed your blog for a long time and have been so interested, delighted and amazed with each and every one of them. I always had the thought that I would write you and make comments, especially on ones that made a great impression on me.

I am nearing the 90 year mark in my life, and I just wanted to let you know that decluttering has pushed me into ridding my house of so much "stuff" that now my children won't have to be concerned about when I move into my final home. Thank you from the bottom of my heart for these wonderful blogs that make an old person look forward to every time I open my computer.

> *Sincerely,*
> *Phyllis*

It's such a beautiful message, and she helped me see new aspects of why decluttering is so great. I hadn't previously thought much about how my stuff will affect the people I love most once I'm gone.

This encouragement doesn't have to be done through a blog or Facebook. I've used everything from Instagram and emails to phone calls and texts to support people in getting rid of clutter.

I've gone into people's houses to help them in person for a day or two. It's amazing how excited I get and how much more research I do before these house visits. For one lady, I wrote quotes that inspire me to declutter and left them on sticky notes around her house to keep her motivated after I left. Seeing the progress in other people's lives makes me want to keep transforming my own.

Benefits of Accountability

Having these routines set up keeps me from going months without thinking about clutter. Instead, it stays in the forefront of my thoughts. People understand if I skip a day of updates or a weekly blog post, but they mention that my message had helped or tell me I should write more. They were in turn encouraging me to keep going even when life got busy for me.

This helped me continue making it a priority. This strategy may not help some people as much as it helped me. **But using it was my**

way of making a difference in others' lives while improving my own.

Because I made decluttering such a big priority, I wasn't doing as much mission-type work, which is also very important to me. So this was my way of still reaching out to help. For others, it may just be about having someone to share the journey with, someone who will notice the difference in their progress.

Accountability also helped me because if I didn't declutter, then I had nothing to share. Many times, I'd get rid of a few items just so I could write a short post about it. Those little things really add up.

While I thought I was just doing stuff to help others, I was really helping myself, too. And their words would come back later to help me even more. Here's one last email from a reader towards the end of a 30-day challenge:

> *THANK YOU!!! I'm doing it...taking interview magazines to a friend with 2 girls to create art and fun for Thanksgiving.*

> *I've had free books on my porch for 2 days and I've met so many neighbors...taking the rest to a free library today. I have a new work area with a cool clean peach desk...yes things are PEACHY.*

> *And very important, I have a wellness area by a painting that inspires me...that use to be piles of books, clothes and randomness that I had not touched for a long time. Thank you Decluttering Coach...Happy Thanksgiving Megan!!!   -A.R.*

I love that excitement especially from someone who is an artist and, like me, used the excuse that she liked big messes and turning junk into works of art. Yet she was able to see how getting rid of clutter improved her life socially, mentally, and physically.

I realize that not everyone has (or *wants*) a blog they can use in this way. But everyone can still create this accountability and help others along the way. Here's a list of things to try. Don't let the list overwhelm you, but do give more than one a try. It might seem at first as if it's distracting you from decluttering, but once you have this system in place, it will keep you going longer than you would have otherwise. I don't consider myself someone who needs a lot of accountability to accomplish a goal because I'm very self-motivated once I see the value in something. Still, these undertakings were surprisingly helpful.

Practical Ideas for Creating Accountability

- Let friends know you want to declutter, and tell them it would help you to have someone to share your successes and struggles with. Ask if they'd be willing to check in with you once or twice a week. It could be a sibling who has no clutter or someone from a mom group you're already a part of who also wants to get rid of more stuff.

- Find a Facebook group about decluttering. I'm in one called KonMari Adventures. It's a great resource for asking others what they've done about a certain item (yearbooks, for instance). Oftentimes, you can just search the group without even having to post your own question because most topics have already been addressed.

- Start your own Facebook group. Even though there are tons of groups already in existence, maybe you just want it to be people you know. It can be a great place to post embarrassing "Before" pictures without all of the internet being able to see.

- Post to your favorite social media that you're reading this book and are looking for someone else who is reading it (or willing to read it). Discuss the book together and work on the same category at the same time.

- Be open with the people who live with you. Tell them why you want to declutter. Don't pressure them to get rid of stuff, but let them know that you think it will improve their lives if you focus on this. Ask them to encourage you, and if there's something else you could encourage them with. When you support them, it will remind you to declutter. It's another way you can give back to others while working towards your own goal.

- Find someone to swap decluttering days with. Go to your mom's house on Mondays to help her, and she can come to yours on Thursdays to help you. Even if you live a few hours away, maybe do the 15th of every month or whatever works with your schedules. You'd be able to have time together while being productive.

- Set a date for a party at your house. Better yet, set up two or three. Start small with a group of people you don't mind seeing some of your mess. Have the second one a month later and invite a few people you'd like to get to know better. Don't plan an extravagant event. It could just be tea and coffee. Having guests is just a way to motivate you by giving you a deadline and something fun to look forward to. The third one could be opening your home to even more people another month later for a birthday party, for example.

Most of all, look for ways to help others with their struggles. When you are constantly pouring out words of encouragement to others, you want to live up to the standards you're trying to get them to reach. It pushes you to do more, too. If you're telling someone else that they can do it and that they need to stop making excuses, you catch yourself when you start to make your own excuses or say you can't do something.

If you take small steps now to do something uncomfortable from the list above, soon it will turn into something effortless. But if you don't change what you're currently doing, then the amount of clutter you have won't change either.

The key is that I used these techniques to actually make progress, which was another important part of becoming clutter-free in less than a year.

Day 13
5-min Task
Create one source of accountability for decluttering. Tell a friend. Join a FB group. Or simply invite someone over.

Fourteen

PROGRESS NOT PERFECTION
{ BUT A *LOT* OF PROGRESS }

"A river cuts through a rock not because of its power,
but because of its persistence."
-Jim Watkins

I know several people who will put off a task because they don't
have time to do it perfectly. I'm so glad I learned early on in my life
that using this method often causes important things to go undone.
I'd rather have something improved than left undone. If I'm
constantly improving even just a little as I have time, then eventually
my goal will be reached. It may not be super perfect, but things can
be impressive and amazing without being perfect.

And in my experience, things can feel perfect even when there are
still flaws. Think of your favorite things in life: your favorite food,
your favorite person, your favorite place. If you paused for a minute
to search for their flaws, you could find some. But you love and
enjoy them anyway. You choose to focus on the good.

That's what I've had to do with my house. I had to realize it doesn't have to be perfect for me to enjoy it and live a lovely life in it. But I also remind myself that it can slowly and continuously get better when I don't put off making small improvements here and there.

A little progress over a long period of time results in more progress than trying to do everything in the few days I have free to devote only to decluttering. Plus, I get burnt out on decluttering that much at one time. My brain starts to shut down and not know what to get rid of. I start staring blankly at all my stuff and end up not getting rid of any more of it. Just like with any goal, I'm not going to reach it if I don't start working towards it. We can put so much thought into getting the timing right for certain goals because we want to be "ready," that we just keep putting them off.

Many people do this with deciding when to have kids. I did this with trying to decide when to get married. And my sister's friend did this with decluttering. She finally realized that there's rarely a perfect time to declutter. There's always something else that could be done first. With having kids, you could say, "Well, I want to travel first or have time to get to know my spouse more." For me with marriage, I wanted to graduate from college and pay off my loans. But once I did those things, I kept setting more goals to accomplish before I got married. There came a point when I realized that I can continue to pursue other goals while I'm married. I guess I felt like I'd stop learning and growing after marriage, so I had to do everything I wanted to before that. I think people view decluttering like that. They see it as something that will take over and disrupt their lives so much that they need to take care of everything else before they start. They see it as draining and time-consuming, so they try to wait until they have lots of energy and enthusiasm about it. Thinking of putting in time and work and still not having it done perfectly can be a major roadblock. Yet the opposite is true long-term: you get more time and energy when you declutter.

As I was sharing my goals on my blog, I didn't tell readers that my house would look like a magazine after I went through every category. Not that I would've had a problem with that.

I wanted there to be huge, drastic change, but I was also realistic. What I *did* tell them was that I'd started following a plan that was helping me let go of stuff for the first time in my life and that I'd love for them to join me if they wanted to do the same.

There was a lot of grace in the beginning because I was just happy to finally be getting rid of my possessions at all.

Measuring Progress

I like to have clients rate their clutter so I can evaluate their progress. When I started seriously getting rid of clutter, I rated it at an 8.5 on a scale of one to ten with ten being the worst. Other people would've probably said an eleven! It wasn't about how other people would rate my clutter, though. I was rating how the clutter *felt* to me. The important thing isn't the number itself but how it diminishes over time. After about six months of serious decluttering, mine was down to a six. After *another* six months of light decluttering, it was down to a five.

That's **huge** for me. That lower number represented how much better I felt about my possessions. What I owned was significantly less overwhelming after that year.

During the next six months, I only focused on it heavily for the equivalent of a week total, and it was down to a four. The thought of moving is already less like a nightmare and more like an opportunity. Since I'll be packing it all up anyway, it'll be easy to get rid of more. I'll never have to deal with decluttering or organizing any of that stuff again. I'll keep reaping the benefits for the rest of my life.

The biggest and best thing I realized was that my clutter no longer overwhelms me.

My clutter level isn't where I want it yet, but it's manageable. I know that I can handle it and get it down to a two without completely interfering with my life. It doesn't stress me out to think of going through my stuff again. Partly because there's less of it, but also because now I know how.

As an artist and a client of mine, Andee Rudloff shares a similar experience. Before she started decluttering, she considered her clutter level a nine. After just a month of decluttering, it went down to a seven. And after a total of about seven months of decluttering, it was down to a four.

Before I started hearing other people's stories, I thought I might be able to move my rating down a point or two in 3-9 months. But five points?! I never would've guessed that. That's a significant difference.

This motivates me so much because it shows that real progress isn't just possible, it's common. And it's worth it. It isn't just for people who have always wanted to be clutter-free.

My sister also experienced how we were raised and vowed to keep a clean house, yet she didn't know exactly how. She did well at maintaining that goal, but it not only exhausted her and her children, it was exhausting for me to watch. It made me want to clean even less than I did before.

After running her own home for fifteen years and having five children, her clutter felt like an eight, especially the garage. It was such a transition for me, of all people, to be giving her advice. Even more surprising, my advice was working, unlike things she'd been trying for years. As a mother, she's always trying to improve and had attended conferences, read books, and shared advice with other moms.

About four months later, she had her clutter down to a three. When she'd found out she was pregnant, she was motivated to make more progress before it became difficult for her to move. Still, even while she was eight months pregnant (as in, she could hardly move or pick up anything or take stuff off for donation) and had lots of stuff for her baby already, her clutter was still at a four, about ten months after starting to seriously declutter.

I texted her when her sixth child was nine months old and asked what her clutter rating was. Her reply? "You're asking on the wrong day. Lol"

But she still said it was only a five! And that the little one did make a huge difference. And she was ready to get back to decluttering!

So again, the major miracle is that she sees it as conquerable. Just the fact that she isn't hopelessly overwhelmed by it is progress. Her home didn't have to be perfect for her clutter rating to be significantly lower than when she started. Now she has the added benefit of being confident that she can fairly easily reduce the clutter again. Even her children have a better ability to declutter now, although they may not be as enthusiastic about it.

She's actually pregnant with her seventh child now. (Is it just me, or does it seem like it's taken me a long time to write this book?) She has just transitioned her children's homeschooling curriculum and has started playing concerts as a family band. Yet even in this crazy time of her life, while the size of her family is expanding and the size of her home is not, her clutter rating has only gone back up to a six or seven. She's still better off than before she started decluttering.

How we rated our clutter over time:	Before	During	After
Me	8.5	6	3.5
My Sister	8	3	6.5
Andee	9	7	4

Another thing that helps me stay motivated to declutter, besides keeping track of how much my clutter is decreasing, is staying in hotels and clutter-free homes. Staying in a clutter-free environment shows me what items are still practical to keep. I experience living without a bunch of extra stuff.

Even backpacking has helped with this. I only had one bowl and one spoon to eat all my meals. I loved it so much that I've continued that practice quite a bit for the last couple of years. I realized how much I can do without in regards to cooking utensils as well.

There are two extremes when it comes to clutter. They can both get to the point that they negatively affect our lives and the lives of those around us. That's why we need to find a balance that works for us.

Day 14

5-min Task

Try a fresh method. Put into practice something you've been wanting to try. Turn around the hangers in your closet, or box up items that have been annoying you and getting in your way. If you don't pull anything out of them in six months—or even three months—donate them.

Fifteen

NOT TAKING IT TOO SERIOUSLY

"Even if you fall flat on your face,
you're still moving forward."
-Victor Kiam

As a full-time nanny of four, I typically used the family's van when picking up the kids. One day, however, I unexpectedly found out that I needed to use my own car.

This wasn't a problem for me. I just had to put some stuff in the trunk and say my least favorite phrase: "Please excuse the mess."

As I suspected, the children weren't thrilled. But at least it gave us something to talk about.

"Wow, your car is, like, rotten!" the six-year-old boy immediately exclaimed.
"Where do I put my feet?" his older sister asked.

I thought surely the next time would be better. They'd be used to it.

"Why don't you clean your car?" It was yet another good question asked by the eight-year-old girl.

I had a list of excuses that clearly weren't good enough for her:

- I don't have time.
- I focus on more important things.
- By the time I get home, I'm tired.
- I travel a lot, so it's nice to have stuff with me. Otherwise I might forget something.
- I don't normally have other people riding in my car, and the mess doesn't bother *me*.

These excuses suited me just fine.

It was more than half a year later before I began thinking, "Maybe I *should* let it bother me. Maybe I should make it a priority and take the time to fix it."

Some moments are more embarrassing now that I look back on them because at the time I wasn't bothered by clutter. And I didn't even think about how it might bother others.

You'd probably think that I'd have more embarrassing stories. But a lot of my clutter stayed hidden from most people by remaining in storage containers or spread out at different family members' houses.

In fact, when I told a lady at my church that I was getting rid of clutter, she said, "You don't need to do that. You don't have a lot of clutter." Boy did I have her deceived! I spent six months doing serious decluttering and still was able to give up more possessions after that.

Although I changed from being a packrat in less than a year as the title of this book suggests, I continue to declutter even now. It's just like someone who gets out of debt in a year. It doesn't mean they stop budgeting or paying attention to their finances.

How Decluttering is like Losing Weight

Decluttering is also like someone who has lost fifty pounds in a year. Even if they've reached their ideal weight, if they've really changed to a healthier lifestyle, they'll continue those new habits. They've become a different person already, but they still have a lot to overcome from years ago. They remain active enough to burn the calories they're still eating. So I must continue removing stuff from my home as I am continually bringing new stuff into it.

It's kind of like a diet for my house. I've never struggled with weight issues. But that's partly because I watched so many other people struggle and fortunately was given the advice to never go on a fad diet but instead make slow, positive lifestyle changes. So that's what I did. I became increasingly interested in fitness and nutrition as I was growing up. It was fascinating, and I could see firsthand that the ideas I learned about were true once I put them into practice.

But my house? It was obese.

And I don't remember getting any good advice about preventing clutter. So I didn't look for ideas on how to overcome it while I was growing up. I didn't get that hunger to learn about it, so I didn't read all the fascinating facts about it until I was out of college.

In order to finally change, not only did I have to start putting less inside my room, but I also had to "burn" the excess weight that was already there, just as people who are losing weight should be actively burning calories, not just reducing their intake. It makes so much sense now that I think of it that way.

It can be such a slow process because it needs to be a sustainable plan. The new energy and strength gained by being free of so many possessions can be subtle enough that it isn't super noticeable. It gradually becomes a new normal.

Just as I see people and don't think of them as being overweight or sluggish, people can see my house and not notice the clutter as much as I do. I might see those same people day after day as they're making healthy changes and still not notice that much of a difference because of that slow progress.

It's the same for me with my clutter. I'm putting in so much time and effort day after day, but just like someone trying to lose weight, I need to pay attention to more than what I'm still dissatisfied with. I need to concentrate on the fact that I feel better. I need to be thankful that my possessions don't take up *as much* space even though my house is still full.

That's how I want someone to be if they're trying to lose weight. **I don't want them to be down on themselves when they've made progress.** That's not helpful. But I have done that very same thing to myself in regards to clutter. I want my friends to celebrate the victory of going down a pants size even if they're the same weight. I want them to use their small progress to spur them on. Once I realized this, I started making a lot more positive comments about my progress with clutter. Self-talk is so important!

When I see a "before" picture of a friend who has adopted a healthy lifestyle, I'm amazed at how different they look. It's often not just their size but also how they talk about the way they feel and what they have energy for. Their excuse is no longer that they're too tired.

Yes, they can still get tired, but they have so much more endurance that they don't get to that point as often.

I've noticed the same with clutter. When I'm in a room full of stuff, my brain gets so busy processing everything that it can be exhausting. But as I've been in places without all that extra stuff, I've noticed how much easier it is to focus and not feel drained as quickly while working on a task.

A Journey of Self-Discovery

When I paid off my debt, I was able to quit working full time so that more of my energy could be spent on different types of work (the kind that don't necessarily provide a paycheck). The same thing happens when we "get out of clutter." We no longer have to focus our thoughts and resources on making sure our "stuff" is taken care of.

Instead, we can spend time making sure our families are taken care of along with only the possessions that are most important to us.

I see it as more than just achieving the goal of having a decluttered house or room. It's more than just a skill. It's a journey of self-improvement and self-discovery. **When you declutter, you're cleaning up more than just your house; you're cleaning up your life.**

I learned discipline and critical thinking by coming up with ways to do what was so against what I'd done my whole life. And I also discovered that some things which used to be important to me don't have to stay with me forever. If I have grown and changed, my stuff should have evolved as well.

Some of my items were surprisingly easy to part with immediately. As I saw patterns emerge, I could tell more about what I liked and what was important to me versus what was not. For example, I realized that I never wore white shirts. Once I saw that they didn't inspire a positive reaction from me, I realized that it was because of how easily they stain or how see-through they are. I know there are ways around that, but I always saw it as extra work. Now that I've gotten rid of them, I haven't even missed them!

I also noticed that I kept getting rid of outfits that had both bold patterns *and* bold colors. I could deal with one or the other, but if it was both, then I didn't feel like it fit my personality. Even though I'm still initially drawn to cute shirts with bold colors and patterns while shopping, I no longer buy them. Another example is that I didn't enjoy wearing tennis shoes. So I got rid of them and didn't replace them even though other people consider them staples of a wardrobe. It wasn't until three years later that I purchased another pair when I switched up my workout routine.

In a way, knowing what I'll use has made me have to be more careful about how much I let myself buy since it's easier to justify buying things I don't need (because I know I'll love and use them).

My favorite and most surprising outcome was how I've been able to help others get rid of their clutter. I actually have advice that has worked not just for me but for them, too.

Now when someone asks a question about clutter, I have a solution. Or I at least know a reliable place to look for one.

Over time, I trained myself to notice clutter and the negativity it brought. This was great while it motivated me to get rid of items that didn't improve my life.

But then something awful happened. Those lovely homes that inspired me to declutter and showed me it was possible in the first place? I began to see the clutter there, too. *Why do they have their bread on the counter? It would look so much better without it. And they should do something with those piles of paper.*

Seriously? I do *not* want to be that person.

Their home is still lovely and peaceful. Having the bread on the counter may be practical and convenient and shouldn't be a concern for me.

There are extremes on both sides of clutter that can be negative.

I want my life and home to be welcoming. Having too much clutter can mess that up, but so can not having any. I have been places where I was uncomfortable because I didn't want to mess anything up because it was so perfect.

And I know people who are obsessive in their cleaning and perfectionism, and they're embarrassed by it. They feel bad for valuing cleanliness over people.

When people apologize for the mess when they only have two things sitting out, I get embarrassed and hope they don't notice my overflowing purse. And then I wonder if I should keep that purse with me at all times so that it doesn't triple the "mess" in their house.

There *is* a balance.

I was reminded of this when I read this passage from *The Thorn Birds* (a novel set in Australia):

> "Since the day I saw this room, I've longed to make it something every person who walks into it will admire, and yet comfortable enough to make every person who walks into it want to remain."

I don't want people to just admire my home. I don't want them to feel like they're out of place or ruining the splendor of the room. I want them to feel like it's an inviting place that's safe from the chaos and criticism of the world.

Just like I've trained myself to be frustrated by clutter after years of embracing it, I can again grow accustomed to accepting the clutter in other people's homes or even what piles up in my own home, without letting it take over my life.

Another thing I had to get frustrated with was debt, and much of what I learned from getting rid of my student loans is also what helped me get rid of clutter.

Also, you should be glad to know: my car is no longer rotten.

Day 15
5-min Task
Write down your biggest excuse not to declutter. Now add a *new* excuse for why you will declutter anyway.

Sixteen

DEBT-FREE TO CLUTTER-FREE

"If you have debt, I'm willing to bet that general clutter
is a problem for you too."
-Suze Orman

Getting out of debt was kind of a letdown. I had expected it to be a bigger deal. I don't regret it by any means, but after accomplishing *any* big goal, my life doesn't suddenly become exactly the way I want it to be. There's always something else to work towards.

I realized that debt hadn't been the only thing I'd accumulated during college. So I took what I'd learned about getting rid of debt and applied it to getting rid of clutter:

Shoot for quick wins.
Debt: To keep from getting discouraged, I put large chunks of my paycheck toward my loan payments so I could watch the numbers drop drastically. Of five loans, I paid off the smallest one with the highest interest rate first. **I kept thinking of all the money I was saving by not paying that extra interest.**

Clutter: **I chose the smallest/easiest room to declutter first (and one that wouldn't immediately accumulate more clutter).** Because of all the paper clutter, it wasn't as fast as I expected. Still, it was faster than a large room with lots of paper clutter. I also filled a bin the size of a toy box with items to donate. I think it only took me a day to fill it that first time because that was my focus. I needed a quick win.

In hindsight, I might've even postponed the paper clutter for later, but it seemed to work alright since I didn't know any better. At least I was doing something!

Make a plan.

Debt: The official student loan repayment plan suggested ten years. I didn't want to be thirty and still in debt, so I set my goal at five years and worked backwards from there. **To pay it off in half the time, I should pay twice the money.** Sometimes I paid more, sometimes less. **Having the plan helped me measure whether or not I was where I wanted to be and make adjustments accordingly.** I ended up paying it off in three years, two whole years earlier than my original plan!

Clutter: I spent about thirty minutes a day decluttering. Again, sometimes more, sometimes less. I usually stop being very productive after about forty-five minutes, especially now that I've gotten rid of most of the easy and obvious stuff. When I do less, it's anywhere from five to twenty minutes. I'm always amazed at how much I can do in five minutes and instantly wonder why I don't do that more often. I almost feel like I get more done when I limit myself to a short amount of time because I don't dawdle or get distracted as much. When I want to do more than forty-five minutes a day, it helps to do one session in the morning, then another that afternoon or evening.

I also have a bin dedicated to items ready for donation as part of my ongoing plan. Having the donation bin helps me:

- measure my progress (I added a sticker to the bin every time the items were bagged up and hauled off.)
- feel accomplished with a quick win each time it's emptied and filled again
- maintain the habit of getting rid of stuff rather than just trying to organize it in a crowded space
- always have a place to put the clutter and know where to find it when I'm ready to donate it (and I also don't get it confused with other boxes)

Be realistic about how long it will take.

Debt: I would have loved to pay off my loans in a year or less, but I knew my lifestyle wouldn't allow that. My paycheck wasn't very big right after graduating from college. I also didn't want to give up my annual trip out of the country because it was the one thing that kept me going. I knew I could pay my loans off in less than 10 years, though, if I kept at it.

Clutter: Before I began, I had naively expected decluttering to only take about three days. Once I began being diligent about decluttering, I recognized that it could be completed in a year. While a whole year seems intimidating, three days is actually more terrifying! **Trying to do everything in a few days made me feel rushed, overwhelmed, discouraged, hopeless, and unprepared.** Instead, I was able to think of how much I can accomplish in a year (without being overwhelmed with the thought that it would never end). It gave me time to develop a system to keep me from letting clutter take over again after it took so much work and time to eliminate.

Implement quickly and consistently.

Debt: I began making payments before they were due. I was never late on a payment (although I came close once), and I regularly made extra payments. **The dollar amount of the payments often varied depending on my job, but the frequency of the payments was solid**. While I only had to make payments monthly, financial decisions occurred more frequently. I made daily decisions about how I'd spend my money: on books? workshops? a road trip? Would I work extra hours for those things or pay less towards my student loans?

Clutter: As soon as I wrote my seven-step plan for a clutter-free life, I started it. Setting up a bin and filling it with donations seemed like a small step, but **a year of repeating that small step did more than a week of big steps**. Sometimes I wished I had done more, but at least I kept doing *something*. I would've gotten discouraged if I'd tried to stay up all night making a dent in the clutter. Instead, I try to do something every day even if I can't do my normal thirty minutes. Maybe I'm out of town and can work on decluttering my email, reading books or articles on simplicity, or making a list of what to do when I get home.

Leave room for interruptions.

Debt: I took weeks and even months off work at a time while paying off loans. I took that into account because it was important to me. I also drove an old vehicle that randomly required financial attention. I didn't let that bog me down. **I remembered that, for the most part, I was paying off my loans quickly**.

Clutter: I prioritize my decluttering by doing it early in the day. If I'm interrupted, I still have time before bed. Some days I wish I'd managed my time better because, before I know it, I'm exhausted and still haven't decluttered. Occasionally I'll still make myself do it, but other times I allow myself to feel that disappointment so I won't let it happen again. I remember that tomorrow is a fresh start. Maybe I can spend extra time on it or just take longer to reach my goal. But **I *will* reach my goal rather than give up because of a bad day here and there**.

Keep an end goal in mind.

Debt: I imagined what paying off my loans in five years would be like. **It would mean more independence and less stress**. I could travel more, quit my full-time job, spend more time with family, start a business, buy land, build a tiny house, start a blog. **I wasn't just paying off student loans because it seemed like a good idea. I had important things motivating me.**

Clutter: **I never wanted to be clutter-free until I realized all the benefits**. I could be a better host and find things quickly when I needed them. Even more surprising was that it gave me more energy as I let go of items I felt obligated to keep (gifts, things "everyone should have"). **I hadn't realized how much mental space my physical clutter was taking up.** Once I found out, I never again considered giving up on a clutter-free lifestyle.

Remember it's hard but worth it (and can even be fun)!

Debt: Going without products other people find so useful can be annoying. For me, it was a laptop. **Even though I wanted to be debt-free more than I wanted my own computer, it was still frustrating** sometimes. It was fun telling people about my accomplishments, though. Not just at the end, but each time I paid off a loan. I love using my story to inspire others and help them reach their own financial goals. And it was really exciting for me to watch the amount I owed dwindle to nothing.

Clutter: Decluttering takes not only physical exertion, but also a lot of mental work. It's a process of decisions. Should this be given to a friend? donated? sold? If so, where? It can be time-consuming and draining. It's exciting, though, when I find an item I can use immediately, like that $100 bill I found in my recipe box. **I've also found several laughter-inducing items because they're so outdated or ridiculous for me to have kept.** It was literally trash from college, like used napkins and an empty box of granola bars that had simply blended in with all the clutter. Who would have ever thought that just like with finances, a girl like me is now able to support others trying to eliminate clutter! I've had fun meeting so many new people, all because of this goal to improve my life.

Decluttering on a Budget

Another way that clutter is related to finances is that people don't want to have to buy things *again* because they decluttered it. I frequently get questions and comments on this topic. Here are a few things I usually say in response to those who are trying to live on a tight budget:

First of all, you're not alone! It's important to consider your budget when getting rid of items. Many times, though, I think we focus on the potential problem of spending money on the same product twice. Meanwhile, we create the bigger and more expensive problem of keeping everything.

Second, we forget that we can live with very little. We can even thrive and be more creative and joyful with minimal material possessions especially for short periods of time. My guess is that if you are on a tight budget it's because you're giving up things for now in order to be better off later. Maybe you won't be able to buy them right away, but you could potentially buy them again a bit later.

My suggestion is to start a donation box in your home. After you've added some clutter to it, leave the box of stuff in your house for a while before donating its contents. This will allow you the time to get used to how the rest of your house looks, feels, and functions without them. If you don't find yourself needing those possessions again for a couple of weeks, they'll be much easier to get rid of.

Lastly, consider whether it's something you could borrow if it ended up being something you really regret not being able to use anymore. Or maybe give it to a friend who would use it more often and let him or her know that you'd like it back if they decide to get rid of it later. You could also tell them that in the meantime you might like to borrow it occasionally.

I realize this can't be done with everything, but putting those suggestions into practice can make a huge impact. And it's okay to keep the other items you feel more strongly about keeping.

The best way for me to be more accepting of whatever decision I end up making or situation I find myself in (even as I work to improve it so it isn't my permanent state) is to focus on what I'm grateful for.

Day 16

5-min Task

Clear the surface. Choose the top of a table, dresser, or nightstand that's been bugging you. You could even choose the surface of the floor in a specific area. Removing items from that surface and put them where they belong. This can make the area so much more relaxing, even if you don't get the entire surface cleared in five minutes.

Seventeen

GRATITUDE

{ HOW IT HELPED ME ELIMINATE DEBT & CLUTTER }

"If you've got a billion dollars and you're ungrateful, you're a poor man. If you have very little but you're grateful for what you have, you're truly rich."
-Sir John Templeton

Paying off $25k in student loans in three years really changed me. It showed me I could reach fairly lofty goals, which helped me believe I could declutter my life once I realized I wanted to. I began to wonder if others had noticed a similar connection between these two lifestyles of being in debt and being cluttered, which both seem to drain the life out of people.

So I asked.

While there were a few who didn't have a problem with either and a few more who only had a problem with one or the other, I was overwhelmed by the responses from those who've dealt with both. Here are some of their thoughts when asked about the correlation:

"The clutter definitely contributes to the debt."

-Debbie B.

"The more progress I make on my debt, the less clutter I have. When the debt pay off slows down, the clutter increases. There is definitely a connection for me."

-Kayla L. H.

"I'm assuming the bills are lost in the clutter, which leads to being in debt?"

-Bobby B.

"The debt, but especially the clutter, gets out of hand and I kind of give in to it."

-Deb. K. F.

Why Do We Accumulate Clutter & Debt?

There were hundreds of similar comments, some even discussing **why we do this to ourselves**. Why do we give in to having clutter and debt?

Did we learn it from our parents? Is it fear of not having enough?

Do we just want to reuse everything we can because we don't want to be wasteful?

Are we too busy to learn to budget? Too busy to get rid of possessions we don't want? Have we believed we can't succeed in getting rid of clutter and debt? Are we overwhelmed? Or just distracted?

Maybe we're free spirits, not bothered much by our debt or clutter. **Do we not even notice it?** Is it our stage of life?

Perhaps we lack adventure and therefore fill our lives with chaos and distractions.

Are we trying to impress others with our purchases (by owning something new or expensive *or* **by showing we're savvy enough to find great deals)?**

Honestly, I can relate to all of these to some extent. Of course there are more reasons for debt that people don't choose, such as high medical expenses.

A question I find more helpful than *why* we have debt and clutter, though, is this …

How Do We Change?

Of the people I asked about the relationship between debt and clutter, here's one last comment I want to share that hints at what plays a key role in helping us change:

> "My husband and I live in a tiny apartment and we try hard to keep clutter out. We have more wins than losses now. I think it's because FPU [Dave Ramsey's Financial Peace University] and paying off debt taught us about contentment." -May B.

She credits learning about contentment. Being content isn't always a natural inclination. It isn't just for people who have always been content or were born with a secret to life. It can be learned. Even better, it can be learned by achieving a worthy goal, such as paying off debt.

It's easy to associate contentment with lack. I often hear contentment mentioned in the context of being content with what we have because we don't have what we want, some situation or item that could benefit us, so instead we should settle for being content without it. I've also heard it used in the sense of someone being content with what they already have and therefore not choosing to pursue a goal they had. It's easier to remain in their state of contentment than to face fears and challenges brought on by their dream.

In reality, contentment *leads* to things that benefit us. It leads us to joy and realizing we already have what we want or can get it in time.

We can be content in the midst of a challenging endeavor or even a season where we lack things we want.

I worked in a therapeutic wilderness program where we shared "gratefuls" before every *meal*. We didn't have internet. We didn't have cellphones or stylish clothes. We didn't even have a toilet. But we still had gratitude.

When all of that "stuff" was stripped away, we were a whole lot more grateful for it. We were also more grateful for something as simple as a warm meal or a nearly empty room.

Exploring Gratitude

My favorite building in America is Thanksgiving Chapel. While exploring downtown Dallas in February of 2014 with a friend from the area, we stumbled upon this building.

The spontaneity of the day allowed us to satisfy our curiosity.

The place looked closed, but we tried the door anyway. I was delighted to find the building empty and quiet. It was such a peaceful place, especially compared to the bustling city. Not only did the atmosphere take my breath away with its uncluttered walls, but so did the surprise I felt when I looked up.

The stained glass ceiling added to the wonder of the chapel.

But it didn't stop there. Where a pulpit might stand in a traditional chapel, there was a table with paper, a pen, and a bowl. It was an invitation to give thanks.

The magic of the moment did not end there either. One of my favorite parts of this experience was reading what others had written and placed in the bowl.

The Power of Gratitude

Whether it's our own thankfulness or someone else's, gratitude does more for us than just pointing us towards contentment. It reminds us we didn't get where we are on our own.

It improves our mood and takes the focus off of whatever is bothering us. It gives our minds a break from worry. That's why I like writing things I'm grateful for every day. God knows I spend time worrying about things nearly every day without even realizing it, so I need to counteract that behavior.

Here are four ways gratitude helped me get rid of debt and clutter:

- Considering that others will be grateful for something I don't even use has helped me get rid of it. That may be done through selling it to pay off debt, but even a donation can benefit us financially. The person I give it to or even sell it to at a reduced price is able to benefit at the same time. *If I have less stuff, I can live in a smaller and less expensive home.*

- Thinking of how grateful I (and my family and friends) would be with an item out of my life, has helped me overcome reluctance in parting with it. Is it hideous? Does it get in the way? *Instead of focusing on all the reasons I wanted to keep it, I had to think of all the reasons I'd be glad it's gone.*

- When I'm using what I have (and am grateful that I have even that much), I'm too busy to miss what I've given up. Complaining about what I don't have or what I "need," wastes a beautiful moment. Sacrificing to get what I want is wonderful, but it isn't much help if I'm complaining about the sacrifice. *I try to be thankful when I get what I want rather than taking it for granted as a need.*

- Gratitude keeps me from impulse spending. Not only have I begun to realize I don't need as much, but I also have a more positive state of mind. This reduces my desire to make purchases just for that shopper's high, which in turn keeps me from future negative feelings associated with buyer's remorse.

When I'm grateful for what I have, I buy fewer items I regret later.

Sadly, there are thousands of people in the Dallas area who have never been to Thanksgiving Chapel. I lived nearby for three months and had never even heard of it. My friend who lived there had no idea it existed.

Imagine how many people walk right by it. Some of them see it. Maybe they even kind of like it. Every day, crowds of people have the opportunity to go there, with very little inconvenience. But they choose something else instead.

Maybe they are constantly choosing something better to do with their time than visit that chapel, but it's more likely that they are missing out on this experience just because they don't know about it. Or maybe it's simply easier for them to go about their day as they usually do.

Now imagine how many people have walked through this entire day without seeing anything to be grateful for. How many see it, but don't take the time to stop and enjoy it and express that gratitude?

Like the people in Dallas, I have the opportunity each day to be inspired by gratitude. I've chosen to stop passing it by. I don't just read about other people's life-changing experiences with it. **I continue to choose to have my own encounter with gratitude.**
I write what I'm thankful for in a journal and make sure to include something unique from the day. I'm always thankful I did, especially when I go back and read them later and have those good feelings all over again!

Gratitude

More than a decade ago, I read a story about gratitude that I've never been able to shake off.

A lady's sister was trying to convince her to thank God for literally everything as the Bible instructs. She wanted her sister to thank God for the lice they had! In the midst of her disgust and discomfort, her sister finally did so, but only begrudgingly.

That lady was Corrie ten Boom.

In *The Hiding Place*, her account of her time during the Holocaust, Corrie wrote that she later found out a reason to be truly grateful for the lice: their lice was the reason the guards of the concentration camp where she and her sister lived, didn't come in their cells to break up the prayer meetings.

No matter how inconvenient or unreasonable thanksgiving may seem, it's always possible and always worth it.

Day 17
5-min Task
Make it sparkle. Find an area in your home that is peaceful, and dust it off. Add a candle or favorite decoration. Maybe even light the candle to make it extra special.

Eighteen

CAR CLUTTER:

{ THE ONE THING THAT WORKED FOR ME }

"Having a disorganized car not only prevents us from feeling comfortable and enjoying the ride, it can also be dangerous. Items rolling around in the vehicle can distract drivers and even cause injury in the event of a sudden stop or crash."
–WeOrganizeU

I'm almost horrified that anyone who has seen my car at a certain period of my life will read this chapter. If they do, they will wonder what right I have to give advice on keeping a car clean.

Yet I think that's why this will be so helpful for other people. If it can work for someone like me who has halfway lived out of their car for the last ten years, then it's worth a try for anyone else struggling in this area.

I will say that it worked wonderfully while I did it. However, it worked so well, that my car stopped being cluttered and so I stopped doing this one thing. Then, over time, my car became cluttered again. So it's more of an ongoing task, but a very simple one that

I've already started implementing in my own life again with much success.

Once I'm out and about, I go back and forth between my car and various destinations. I'm someone who loves to stay home, so I might be getting in and out of my car even less frequently than most people throughout the week.

But it still seems like a lot: every time I leave my house, the grocery store, or the mall, every time I get gas, every time I leave work. Throughout the day, if I'm going back to a messy car, **that's how many times I'm being inconvenienced by it.**

Maybe I have to move stuff around to put the groceries in or to fit guests in my car. Maybe I'm embarrassed because people nearby can see all the trash I have. (My dad once said jokingly, "If you want a clean car...litter!") **Maybe it's just a reminder of one more thing I need to do.**

While I don't do a lot of driving during the typical week, I frequently take four-hour road trips to visit family and friends. **I often feel like I live out of my car.** When I put something in it, I'm very tempted to leave it there because "I'll probably need it again by next week anyway."

However, that mentality has caused my car to become more and more cluttered. During the few occasions when my car has been completely decluttered, I enjoyed the feeling of seeing nothing in the seats or floorboards. Once I get it to that point, I'm more likely to work harder to keep it that way.

So the first step for me is always to start by remembering how nice it was to see a clutter-free car. Even when I couldn't remember a time that my car was clutter-free, I was able to think of how nice it was to get in a friend's clean car. That usually gives me the motivation I need to start my one thing for getting, and keeping, my car clutter-free.

But, unlike in my room, it works better in regards to my car if I just do one thing at a time. If I try to set aside a big chunk of time, I find a reason to avoid it.

I used to think, "Okay, if I set aside one day a week to spend 30 minutes decluttering the car, that'll make such a big difference."

But now, it's a routine I'm not even interested in trying. In the past, I've always run into the problems of something else coming up, bad weather, or just not being in the mindset for it that day. But really, I also just forget what day it is half the time!

These are excuses I have yet to work through. In the future I might think it's the best plan ever and wonder why I didn't implement it sooner. But with some things (like a capsule wardrobe, which I'll discuss in another chapter), I have to be ready for it or it won't work.

Usually when we're getting in the car, we're in a hurry. When we're getting out of the car, we're tired from a long day of work or traveling. When we're in the house, we're focused on what's going on inside and not thinking about our car.

So here's the #1 thing I did to get and keep
my car cleaned out:

*I took something with me every time I got out of
the car.*

This is pretty effortless, but also very effective. It's easy to make it a habit because it's so simple. It's easy to remember, which means it's more likely to happen.

If I'm exiting my car at a restaurant, gas station, or shopping center, I grab a piece of trash, even if it's just a straw wrapper, or a whole bag of trash when I have it. If I'm at home, I grab a jacket or pair of shoes to take inside with me.

Establishing this habit makes a huge difference. **I'm not having to make several trips back and forth to the car** in addition to what I regularly do, like when I have groceries. **Instead, I take just one extra thing each time I'm already walking from the car to the house.** And I don't have to feel guilty when I don't take more with me because I know I'll grab other stuff next time.

Does taking one thing out sometimes turn into taking two or three? Yes, but only when it's manageable. That part is flexible. One is the minimum, and anything else is just extra because I want to.

This method also keeps things from piling up in my house. It's easy to put one thing away at a time. But if I take everything from my car inside at one time, I might be exhausted or distracted before I have a chance to put it all away.

This has helped me so much. Once I've made it a habit, it means I'm looking for and noticing the clutter in my car instead of trying to block it out. It means **I'm being aware of decluttering more often, which can remind me to declutter other areas of my life as well once I go inside my house.**

Honestly, my car still doesn't always look decluttered, but it's definitely a lot easier and faster to get it that way since I've implemented this habit.

However, here's the next best thing I did to keep my car clutter-free once I had the first habit established:

I started using three containers.

It seems really basic, but when I have a container for the stuff that inevitably piles up in my car, then it isn't sliding around as much while I'm driving.

First, I use a bag for trash, usually a grocery bag (or even a cup from a fast food place).

I keep this in the front so I can always reach it. Some people like hanging it over the back of the passenger seat.

Second, I keep a medium-sized box in the backseat. This container holds items that are in my car temporarily: something I want to return to a friend or items I just bought. Instead of being in denial and thinking I'll always keep everything out of the car, I've embraced it and made a place for those extra things.

Once this container gets full, I know it's time to take care of those items. I can easily take the box in the house and put the items where they belong. But for the days I'm in a rush, at least it's easy to move stuff around so people can ride with me. Or if I'm getting my car serviced, I can move those things to the trunk easily so the rest of the car can be vacuumed.

Third, I have a large box in the trunk which I use for items I like to permanently keep in the car (because I enjoy spontaneous sleepovers and camping trips). I'll also put a box of stuff to donate in the trunk if I'm not going that day but want to make sure I have the box with me when I do go (since the closest place for me to donate is about forty-five minutes away).

It helps for me to **imagine how much more pleasant it'll be to get in my car throughout the day and not wonder what others are thinking when they see it.** I'm more likely to put the "one thing" into practice if I think about how nice it is to not have to clean the car out before letting someone ride with me. **When I focus on a future vacation and the idea of not having to spend twenty minutes moving stuff around so I have a place to put my luggage, I get really motivated to use the "three containers" regularly.**

While I've struggled almost constantly with car clutter, the results of changing my habits were astonishing and well worth the minimal effort I put in. The kitchen, on the other hand, is what I love getting organized. I will gladly put a lot of time into getting it the way I want it. The stories I'll share next include the changes that made the biggest difference in the houses I've worked in over the years.

Day 18

5-min Task

Take and share After pictures! Go around your house to take pictures of the decluttered areas or even of your Donation Station or the chart of all you've gotten rid of so far. Share it with a friend or FB group.

Nineteen

KITCHEN CLUTTER:

{ RECIPES AND CONTAINERS AND GADGETS, OH MY! }

"Don't own so much clutter that you will be relieved to see your house catch fire."
- Wendell Berry

I get lots of questions from readers about their kitchens. The kitchen is constantly in use, and they don't want to take the time to organize it, much less declutter. Who has time for organizing when there are dishes piling up in the sink and on the table?

While organizing my own kitchen, I learned that I need to do what works for me and not just what I've always seen done. I try new ideas frequently. If they don't work for me, I change them again. There isn't just one way to set up a kitchen. What worked for me in the past might not fit my current lifestyle. And what works for someone else might be totally wrong for the way my brain functions. Keep all this in mind as you read this chapter.

There's a lot going on in the kitchen, so let's start with recipes.

Recipes

Sorting through paper recipes may be the most dreaded decluttering task of all, but for me it is the simplest. For those of you like me who use recipes each week, it can make the biggest difference.

The thought of organizing my sister's recipes stressed her out for the longest time. She kept postponing and avoiding it because it was too daunting. My sister had six kids to cook for and was overwhelmed by the thought of going through all the recipes she'd accumulated. But once my mom recruited me to organize her own recipes, my sister kept hearing about how much my mom was enjoying the benefits of having them organized. My sister was so excited to find that it wasn't a multi-day project. It seems like it would take a long time, but in my experience, two or three people can knock it out in less than two hours.

Since we weren't doing this task alone, it was fun to chat about the different recipes we came across that we wanted to try or that we remember enjoying.

So here's the process we went through:

1. We chose a two to three hour block of time. The amount of time this takes may differ depending on the number of people or recipes. We didn't have anywhere to be the day we did this, so even if it had taken longer, we would have been able to get the scattered recipes back in place before bed. We had the option of working on it longer if we'd needed to.

2. We worked on this as a team. My sister had her fifteen-year-old daughter and me there to help her. She was able to delegate a

lot of the tasks involved. Although my niece and I didn't know which recipes she wanted to get rid of, this task was more about organizing the recipes in order to make them easier to declutter a different day on her own. Typically I focus on decluttering first, but if we don't already have recipes organized, then decluttering them seems overwhelming. That's because we feel the need to declutter all of them at once so we can put them away without forgetting which ones we'd gone through already and which ones we hadn't. After they're organized, then we can go through one category per day or per week to get rid of the recipes we don't use or want.

3. We chose categories as we went. Just as my sister had different categories than I would have, so your categories will probably be different. But here is a sample list of categories we ended up using: meat dishes, pasta/rice/breads, breakfast, Mexican, dessert, chili/soup. We found many recipes that fit multiple categories. So we put those in the categories where we thought we'd look for them first. I was easily able to place most recipes in the best category for my sister or mom, but it was good for them to be around during the process so they could answer questions that arose.

4. We made simple labels. We used flash cards or even pretty cardboard we already had at the house. We could have even labeled them in a binder. There are plenty of options. What's most important is that they got labeled *that day*. We can always make it fancier later when we have more time, but since there's so much other clutter to deal with, that wasn't a top priority at the time.

5. We put the recipes away and enjoyed being able to quickly find them (instead of searching and searching only to call a friend or family member to give it to us). My sister had tried to organize her recipes before, but she was trying to put them in alphabetical order! It became a real problem when she couldn't remember the exact names of recipes. And while we were reorganizing them, my niece found "Cream Cheese Squares" under the letter Z.

Containers for Leftovers

One of the biggest things that drives me crazy is a drawer of lids. Even if there's a container somewhere else in the kitchen that goes with each lid, it takes forever to find a match.

While I was working as a nanny, I realized there was another way. That family had sets of similar containers—either with the lid on it while in storage or with the similar lids stacked together beside their containers.

I never even noticed until later that the family I worked for didn't have any random empty butter or yogurt containers waiting to be reused. I used to think it was so economical to keep them, but now I don't find them to be practical. Those containers are deceptive and confusing because the label no longer accurately describes what's inside. Is it leftovers, and you need to add yogurt to your grocery list? Or will your kids have to open it looking for leftovers only to find the packaging was correct, and the container does still have yogurt in it?

It may seem like a small thing, but I like having containers that I can see through. (Plus, those big white yogurt containers are usually fairly ugly.)

My mom had a drawer of lids, so I went through all of her containers and informed her that I was only keeping the ones that had both a lid and a container that formed a match. There was a surprising amount that we were able to get rid of guilt-free. Then we placed the tops on their containers, and since we'd gotten rid of the others, they all still fit in the cabinets. The "throw-away" type of containers we kept are used when sending food home with someone since she doesn't care if she gets them back or not.

We bought several containers we were excited about at a yard sale for about fifty cents each for her own leftovers.

I've honestly been amazed at how she's kept this system going for over three years now. It saves so much time and avoids frustration. I hated rummaging through those things before and sometimes never even finding a match!

Now, even if they're in disarray, it's easier because there are fewer things to try matching together. Plus, I at least know they all have a match and searching won't be a wasted effort.

This type of used plastic food container is a good place to start in the kitchen because they aren't pretty nor do they have sentimental or monetary value. If you find that you have a use for one, you'll probably already have a nearly-empty one in the fridge at any given time. Just eat the last of the yogurt, and then use its container.

Kitchen Gadgets

I have a reader who wrote to me that she'd spent lots of money on nifty gadgets for her kitchen and didn't want to get rid of them even though she only used them occasionally. She didn't want to buy another one every time she wanted to use it again.

She brought up some great points that are pretty common. In college, I sold Pampered Chef products for a while. I didn't have a dishwasher in my apartment, so I found that, even though I loved certain products, I *didn't* love washing them by hand. But I was glad I didn't have a dishwasher so that I didn't accidentally put something in it that wasn't dishwasher safe.

All of that to say this: how much joy a dish creates is determined by more than just its main function or how it looks. Sure, I've had things that helped me cook part of my meal faster, but then I had to spend extra time cleaning it or taking all the pieces apart. In the long run, it wasn't saving as much time and trouble as I thought it would.

When you use a small item only once a year—a thermometer for a turkey, for example—keeping it doesn't impact your kitchen much.

Having cabinets full of items that only get used a few times a year, however, *can* have a negative impact on using your kitchen the rest of the year. Is that worth it? Each person has to decide for themselves. But if we really want to be clutter-free, getting rid of those items is a step toward making that happen. If it's missed that much, it can be bought again with the knowledge that we want to keep it. We wouldn't be buying it just for the one time and then selling it or giving it away every year. However, we might find that *not* having those things is worth the extra effort involved in preparation those few times a year.

A good way to handle seasonal gadgets is to first figure out how much space to allow for those items. Maybe it's one cabinet or one box or one shelf, or maybe it's whatever can line the back of the cabinets. I've even thought about arranging it by season and having a box of spring/summer items, for example, if that's the only time I make lemonade and use a juicer. Then for fall/winter, I could move that to the out-of-the-way spot and put the cold weather items where I have better access to them, much like the process some people use for clothing.

Doing this will help us notice if we're saying "yes" to more than we'd like. It'll help us prioritize.

It also makes sense to have these items stored in a less convenient area to get to—an area that's very high or low since these items won't be used daily. This process allowed me to stop checking every drawer and rummaging through them, wondering which drawer I put the can opener in. With fewer items in each drawer, it's easier to remember where each item is or at least see everything at a glance once I open the drawer. Putting frequently-used serving spoons and spatulas in a vase on the counter also helps with this while at the same time keeping them within reach.

When I have time for it, I love cooking. I get excited about the whole process: deciding what delicious food to have, making a grocery list, buying the groceries, putting them away, preparing the ingredients, adjusting the recipe, and eating of course!

Occasionally I even enjoy doing the dishes—especially if a friend is helping or the water warms my hands on a particularly cold day.

All in all, it's a lot of work even if it is fun. Since so much time is spent in the kitchen, I try to put items in places that make sense to me. Obviously, this might not be the same for everyone, but for people who spend lots of time in the kitchen, simplifying it can make a huge difference.

Trouble opening and closing drawers because they are too full is a fairly easy fix. It *can* (and should) change by decluttering. It's a great way to remove some frustration from our lives.

If my family has pots and pans stacked more than two or three high, it's a fight for me to get to the one I want. The same can be true if I'm trying to get cookware from the back of a bottom cabinet—it's loud and annoying. It no longer seems wasteful to leave that space empty (or at least put the once-a-year stuff there, which makes for far fewer annoyances when I only have to do it a few times a year rather than once or more a week).

Next, I'll explain how I use a simple seasonal method for my clothes by narrowing down my wardrobe in a way that worked for me (instead of trying to select an arbitrary number of clothing items recommended online), and how this method of organizing my clothes changed my everyday life.

Day 19
5-min Task
Load the bags and boxes from your Donation Station into your car. Don't forget to count them and mark them on your chart!

Twenty

MY HUGE CAPSULE WARDROBE

"I'm nicer when I like my outfit."
-Anonymous

While I recommend starting the decluttering process with clothing, I do not recommend going so far as to make a capsule wardrobe until the clothes are to a manageable amount. A capsule wardrobe was my last major decluttering change.

For those of you who haven't heard of a capsule wardrobe, TheEveryGirl.com defines it as "a mini wardrobe made up of really versatile pieces that you completely LOVE to wear." It's a minimal amount of clothing to wear over the course of three months. After that, you rotate out some of your clothes that no longer fit the season of the next three months. Then you add in the same amount that you took away.

Some of the blogs I read mentioned buying new items to complete the wardrobe. That got me worried and kept me from trying it for a while because I didn't want to spend extra time or money on it. It turned out that I didn't even need to buy anything for my first capsule wardrobe because I already had so many clothes.

When I first heard of a capsule wardrobe, I remember thinking it was *extreme*. I'd just be happy to fit all my clothes in one closet.

After six months of decluttering by getting rid of anything I wasn't thrilled about, all of those little tricks I'd read that never made sense to me in the past started actually working for me. I was able to focus on getting rid of one or two items every time I got something new— and it made a noticeable difference.

I had the time and energy (and not too many clothes) plus the desire to turn my hangers around in my closet. This enabled me to see what clothes I put off wearing and figure out why or just get rid of them.

When I reached the point where I could count each article of clothing without feeling like it would take up too much time (as in, more than half a day), I discovered that I had a manageable amount that I could fairly easily turn into a capsule wardrobe. Before, counting everything seemed wasteful because I thought my time would be better spent getting rid of stuff.

And it was.

Transitioning to a Capsule Wardrobe

As I mentioned above, I didn't go from packrat to capsule wardrobe right away. I was about a year into seriously decluttering before I felt like attempting it. Initially, the idea of trying it myself was both exhilarating and terrifying. It didn't seem like something I was ready for. It was more of a distant, foggy dream.

Yet as I kept hearing about it, I warmed up to the idea and couldn't stop thinking about it. *I saw it less as a super-human task for the elite and more like a practical lifestyle change.*

After decluttering my clothes thoroughly for a month and then continuing to get rid of more throughout the rest of the year, I realized that a capsule was actually within my reach. I had heard of several different ways of doing a capsule wardrobe, which helped me realize that **I didn't have to follow someone else's rules precisely in order for it to benefit me.**

The capsule wardrobes I've seen have been about thirty to forty clothing items for three months. This includes shoes, tops, bottoms, dresses, and light jackets–*not* accessories, PJs, undergarments, or workout clothes. Instead of stressing myself out by only choosing forty items or less for the next three months, I chose very selectively the items that I wanted to wear for the upcoming season. The total ended up being fifty-eight items, and I was okay with that. It seemed like so much in comparison to other people who do capsule wardrobes, but it was still much less than I had before.

I'm pretty sure I had over twenty pairs of jeans to begin with, and hardly any of them even fit me very well. After creating my capsule wardrobe for the first time, I had it down to six pairs of jeans. (Even after a couple of years, it's stayed at about seven pairs with little effort. And now it's down to just two after a couple more years.) After my initial decluttering of clothes, **I purged my wardrobe again, making a pile for "one last wear"** (clothes that I wanted to wear again before I got rid of them in case I decided they look better on me than I thought). That gave me a whole extra section in my dresser! I no longer even take the time to wear everything from my "one last wear" pile one more time. Still, I don't think I could've gone directly to giving them away without that step of giving myself permission to wear them again first.

The next thing that helped me start a capsule wardrobe is that I realized it was no longer unmanageable to count how many articles of clothing I had.

Not including dirty clothes or summer clothes I'd already moved to the back of the closet (which would've added about thirty each), I had one hundred and thirty-one items (nearly two hundred items total)! I decided I'd be happy just getting that down to one hundred within the year.

That was all of the preliminary work, which I'd wanted to do for a while anyway. The rest is what I did in one day:

The next time I was home, **instead of just grabbing what I could get rid of, I made a pile of the items I definitely wanted to wear that winter.**

I didn't get rid of all my summer clothes or even put them in storage. Both of those create huge tasks at one time (either buying lots of clothes or hauling bins around and re-washing stuffy clothes).

Plus, I already have my summer clothes down to my favorites and am looking forward to wearing them again! I live in the South, too, which means it could be in the eighties or higher on some winter days.

I still want access to all of my clothes since this is my first attempt at a capsule wardrobe, but I have them in different sections of the closet. This way I'm only looking at a small percentage of my clothes each morning as I'm getting ready. This makes it much easier and faster to find an outfit that fits the weather and my mood. If I can't find what I need there, *then* I can look in the other section.

The two sections I made in my closet:

1. **Clothes for the next three months.**
2. **Clothes for the rest of the year.**

My total for the next three months is about fifty-five (I'm still adjusting items here and there).

Having fewer clothes has eliminated a large chunk from the decision-making process, but it still leaves room for creativity and variety based on the day's activities.

One of the drawers I'd emptied while decluttering is now used for storing summer shoes. I'm pretty excited because in three months it will feel like I get to go on a free shopping spree of items that fit me perfectly and are my favorite styles!

Here are my thoughts after about two months of using a capsule wardrobe:

I've now worn every article of clothing that I'd originally chosen for the wardrobe. I've only added about five items that I had in the other section of my closet. However, I've also gotten rid of about the same amount. Some items I previously thought I loved, ended up not being as fantastic as my other favorites. **It was easy to see that they were unnecessary because I knew exactly what articles of clothing I'd still have left.**

I made my first clothing purchase since before I started the capsule wardrobe. Karin of TruncationBlog.com inspired me to buy a pair of red shoes because red is the only color she has in her current wardrobe besides neutrals.

I had noticed that I frequently wanted a different pair of flats other than the two pairs I have, and often it was for outfits that could use a splash of color.

The fun of getting dressed each day has increased the more I've used the capsule wardrobe rather than getting boring like I'd thought it might. Now I have the added bonus of actually wearing all the clothing I own.

As I write this, it's been two years since I started my capsule wardrobe. I haven't been as diligent with it, but I also haven't needed to be. That's partly due to the fact that, for five months, I was wearing a work uniform which consisted of work t-shirts almost every day. During that time, I didn't really get to have fun with my wardrobe. Even though my wardrobe needs a tune-up, it's still quite functional the way it is. I'm still benefiting from the work I did years ago, even without putting much work into it lately. Those are the kind of changes I like to share with people, rather than a bunch of quick tips that cause everything to end up in chaos again a few months later.

I do still keep my clothes much more limited and somewhat more organized by season than I used to. I've started reaping the benefits again now that I don't have to wear a t-shirt every day for work. As I'm getting rid of clothes again, I've stopped telling myself that I like variety and started reminding myself that **I like consistently fabulous clothes even more than a variety of pretty good clothes.** One of my favorite things about only keeping my favorites is that I only wear my favorites. So I feel a lot more confident about what

I'm wearing. Sometimes my only excuse for not wearing an outfit was that it was too dressy. But now I wear it anyway since it's the only thing I have clean or haven't worn yet.

Having a capsule wardrobe has really kept my clothes under control at every stage from laundry (there can't be a pile of 100 dirty clothes since I only have 55 items I'm wearing per season) to getting dressed each day. I've mentioned that I'm not a super decisive person. A capsule wardrobe eliminates more than half my clothes as options when I'm choosing an outfit. That's some great practical help!

Because we're constantly wearing clothes and changing clothes, it affects more than we realize. People who have kids can see very quickly what a difference a large amount of clothing can make. And with children, they are growing out of clothes so quickly that it can be a huge task to maintain and organize that process. It's nice once they are old enough to help, but then the question I always hear is how to get them to help.

Day 20
5-min Task
Write yourself a note to remind you to drop off donations next time you're in town. Put it on the driver's seat so you see it next time you get in the car. While you're there, grab one thing to remove from the car.

Twenty-One

TEACHING KIDS TO DECLUTTER

"Organized clutter is still clutter."
- Corie Clark,

The Simplicity Project

Just as *I* don't enjoy being overwhelmed with daunting decluttering tasks, neither do the children I work with. Over years of babysitting, I've also noticed that the way kids' toys pile up isn't much different than how my possessions added up and started taking over the house. In many ways, the solution is also the same. (If you don't have kids, these ideas are still helpful for yourself or a roommate.)

I've often been asked by parents how they can convince their kids to part with their possessions. My basic answer is to try inspiring them to declutter more than forcing them (which creates a negative experience that they don't want to repeat). Think about what inspires you to get rid of your stuff.

Instead of just saying, "We're gonna do this because I want a clean house," say, "We're going to try making our home more welcoming for our family and friends and even ourselves." Ask if they enjoy having visitors over. I've heard so many stories of children who really enjoyed all the space they had for playing once they got rid of stuff.

Show them how it would be easier on them, how they wouldn't have to rush or spend a whole day (or week) just getting their room ready for company. Sure, it may still look like a disaster sometimes when their toys are out and scattered, but it's much faster to get everything out of the way when it all has a place.

Introducing Kids to a Clutter-Free Lifestyle

- **Teach the benefits of decluttering.** Teach your kids that it's a valuable life skill that will benefit them and those they love for the rest of their lives. Share the joy and freedom it enhances. (I say that it *enhances* because I had plenty of joy even when I had clutter, and a lack of clutter doesn't automatically produce overwhelming joy and freedom.)

- **Explain the tasks in ways they can understand.** Let them know how much time you want them to put into it. This depends on the stage of your child's development, but I'd say anywhere from five to twenty minutes is a good starting point. Tell them why they're doing this. (It can give them room for more stuff later, such as on birthdays or holidays. It'll make cleaning their rooms faster. It makes it easier to find things. There's more room to play or be creative.)

- **Help them set small goals and work their way up.** Day one might just be a day of discussing the benefits, tasks, and goals and then getting them set up to start the next day. You could tell them that if they happen to find something to put in the donation pile, they can go ahead but that you don't require them to start until the next day. Day two could involve a challenge to fill the box or get rid of X number of items (ten?). Day three could be for them to go through one category of clothing (all of their shirts or all of their pants or all of their shoes, etc) or get rid of 11 items or work for fifteen minutes instead of ten (less if they're much younger).

- **Show them that it can be fun.** Yes, I know kids who will still complain (or complain even more) if you try to act like what you're making them do is fun. Over time, though, they sometimes come around. And if it works for one kid, that's still better than nothing. One way to do this is by simply changing your wording. You could give it a fun name instead of calling it cleaning time. I've recently realized that lots of people have a name for their cluttered areas, such as "the abyss" or "the dungeon." You could say, "It's time to save stuff from the black holes! Let's see if we can fill the space ship (donation box) in ten minutes." I feel silly just typing that, but sometimes even if kids think it's super cheesy, turning it into a game and being a little dramatic helps *me* have more fun teaching them to declutter. You could also try to see how many items they can add to the box in ten minutes. Maybe even write it down to see if they can beat that number next time.

- **Get them started.** Supply them with a box or bag to put items in for donation. Make sure they have a trash can so they can also get rid of things that aren't worth donating. Tell them it's best to start with larger items because it makes a noticeable difference faster. Trashing a piece of paper won't put as much of a dent in the clutter as getting rid of a big stuffed animal. (But don't discourage little stuff, either. I don't mean they should ignore a piece of paper they come across and know they don't want.) However, if stuffed animals are their most prized possessions, start with other items that they don't use anymore. Give them time to adjust to the idea of letting go before you have them select a stuffed animal or two to part with. They may see how many their friends have and think that they themselves don't have enough. This is a good way to introduce a discussion about people who don't have an abundance of toys.

- **Be prepared for them to want to get rid of things you don't want them to get rid of.** Maybe you paid a lot for it or it's great quality or has sentimental value for you. At that point, they've done the work and should reap the benefits. Maybe find a family member who would also find it sentimental. Or put it in your own room or in the attic until another child can use it. If you aren't willing to keep it among your items, maybe it isn't as valuable as you thought. Try not to force them to keep too much in their room even though they've said it doesn't add joy to their lives. That will discourage them to keep going because they'll think you might overrule them about more stuff, so they're just wasting their time trying to get rid of clutter. Letting them choose what to get rid of is a part of letting them grow up.

It's great to go ahead and teach your children these things early so they know how to do them when they're out on their own as well.

A girl I babysat used to talk about her mom being OCD. She'd complain about always having to clean. One day, she got home from a sleepover and immediately thanked her mom. Her friend's house had been so crowded with junk that it was uncomfortable. The 14-year-old girl I babysat hadn't appreciated how relaxing her own house was until she saw how other people live.

Tips for Making the Process Easier

My sister's daughters were really involved in choosing which clothes to get rid of, but her sons didn't care much. So for the boys, we went through all of their clothes and took out the ones we thought didn't fit or had too many holes or stains. Then we had them look through only the clothes we were going to give away to make sure they didn't want to keep any of them. They did decide to keep some, but we were still able to get rid of a lot.

Even for me, I recently chose one bookshelf to go through and select which books I definitely knew I wanted to keep. Then it was much easier to tell myself that I must not really want to keep the others because they aren't in my "definite keepers" pile. So I boxed up two-thirds of the books on the shelf to sell at the bookstore! And I seriously love books. Like, if anyone else had told me a few years ago that they were doing that, I'd have said they weren't really a book lover. Believe me, I love books! I mean, I'm even writing one. So this might be a good task for your kids to try in order to quickly get rid of items on a shelf.

Another common question I get is about toys. First, think about how you'd feel if your kids decluttered your stuff for you based on what they value. Imagine what they'd keep and what they'd get rid of! Your important possessions are in many ways simply toys. They entertain you or allow you to connect with friends. They give you a mission or purpose. That's how important children's toys are to them because their toys serve those same functions. Keep that in mind as you allow them to make more of the decisions about what they keep and get rid of. Maybe even make it a game where they get to tell you what items of yours they'd get rid of!

5   Ways to Keep the Toys Under Control

1. If you have a donation bin, try to keep it in the same spot
    so that your children always know where it is and can add
    to it anytime. (If you still don't have one, I recommend
    setting one up. It can be really small and pretty, or big and
    out of the way.) **This consistency alone is great, but it
    can be even better if you take them with you to drop off
    the donations so they can see the interaction that takes
    place.** They'll have a chance to see it go to a person,
    whether it's someone you know or an employee at a thrift
    store.

2. **Make sure you talk to your kids about the benefits of
    donating.** It's so valuable because it's a way to help other
    people afford something they want. The toys they don't use
    anymore can find a new home where they do get played
    with and might become someone else's favorite toy.

3. No matter how many toys they get rid of, if they continue
    getting more then the chaos is also going to continue.
    Instead, start to let family and friends know that you're
    trying to limit their gifts. If a grandmother particularly
    loves giving gifts, ask if she could keep some of them at
    her house (like the ones that annoy you the most or make
    the biggest mess at your house). Even easier, stop getting
    as many toys for them yourself. **Try giving experiences
    instead. Ask them what they'd like to _do_ for their
    birthday instead of what they _want_.** Or even give them
    items that will be used up quickly, like snacks.

4. It can go a long way for you to let your children see how
    you practice all of these things. **Your kids learn from
    seeing you get rid of a few items to make room for one**

you want even more. Christmas can be a great time for them to practice it themselves. They're already out of school for the holidays, so they have more time. In addition, they're excited about what gifts they might receive, which can be really motivating for them to get rid of other items to make room in the toybox or on the shelf for the new ones.

5. **Train them to put what they just finished playing with away before they take out a new toy.** This will serve them well in their adult lives, too, but you'll also reap the benefit of it now. There are entire books written about how it's better to focus on one thing at a time rather than going back and forth between projects.

Using these practices has made a big difference in my own life. **While children may not be as motivated or enthusiastic about doing these tasks as you'd like, every little bit helps.** Besides, if they don't even know that it's a problem or how to fix it, they're a lot less likely to help. Keep trying, and over time, the slow progress can really add up.

There's no need to rush them to do it all at once, because over time you'll see the progress they're making. However, occasional decluttering sessions may be necessary so they can quickly see a big difference in how much space they have for all the creative activities they enjoy.

Besides reducing how many possessions they receive as gifts, another good tactic for maintaining is to make them aware that things can pile up again. Have a discussion about how they'll need to get rid of something every time they get something new or else they'll be stuck doing the entire process over again. If they don't go into it knowing this, then they'll be more likely to push back and say decluttering doesn't work when you try to get them to do it again.

This chapter is here to get you started, but if you're interested in reading more on this topic and finding more in-depth information for a specific age, a quick search on Google can lead you to some of the most respected experts on the topic of decluttering (such as Joshua Becker of Becoming Minimalist, Marie Kondo with her KonMari Method, and Leo Babauta of Zen Habits).

Not only will you be thankful you taught them how to manage the amount of possessions they have, so will they…eventually.

I talk a lot about being sentimental about the future to help get rid of things from my past, but don't get me wrong—I'm still me. I still have some items from my childhood. But next, I'm going to explore what has stayed the same versus what has changed since I started decluttering. I'll also share some of the deeper issues I had to deal with when learning to let go of things from the past so I could enjoy a better future.

Day 21

5-min Task

Relax and enjoy. So often we're quickly onto the next thing. Take the time to soak in the peace of a newly clutter-free area of your home for five whole minutes.

Twenty-Two

WHAT WAS I AFRAID OF?

"What are fears but voices airy?
Whispering harm where harm is not."
- William Wordsworth

Until I started getting rid of it, I didn't think clutter had anything to do with fear, and I certainly didn't think those fears had anything to do with my self-worth. But as soon as I would get ready to let go of something, I'd panic. *What if I need it later? Will I be okay without it? What if people don't like me because I no longer have one of these?*

Yet there were even deeper fears that went along with getting rid of my possessions. *What if I'm not good at managing my possessions even after I try getting rid of most of them? What if I spend years getting rid of stuff, and it's all a waste because it goes back to being cluttered again? What if I don't like who I am anymore once I'm clutter-free?*

These questions almost seem silly to me now. It's like I was doubting that any good thing was in my future. My mindset was that my past held the best years of my life. Even though I didn't earn every good moment in my past, it almost felt like I had to earn every single one in my future. When I feel like I'm not good enough to deserve anything, I have to hold onto every little thing I already have. It's a terrible way to live when I think about it that way!

It's especially crazy because the things I was afraid of didn't even happen. I love who I am now. Getting rid of my clutter has only improved that. I'm not a completely different person; I'm just a better version of myself. And my friends didn't run away because I was getting rid of my stuff. They encouraged me and were inspired by my decision, follow-through, and example.

And what if I need something later? Then I'll do what's necessary to get it again *later*. It really isn't a big deal. I should've been afraid of what I'd lose by keeping everything. I had to start making myself afraid of the cluttered person I'd become if I kept adding more possessions without disposing of any.

Yet, while I like my life more than before, and I wouldn't go back to a cluttered me, I want to make one thing clear. I don't love the people in my life any more or less based on how much or how little they own. And my friends and family don't love me any more than they did before just because I have less clutter.

Whether you have clutter or not, you have value. If you try to declutter a thousand times and fail, you still matter. If people don't like you because you don't own a particular item, you're still important. If you get rid of something that you can't ever replace and you regret it for the rest of your life, you are still loved. If someone gets frustrated with you because you have too much stuff, you are still an amazing person. If you feel scatterbrained because of all you have going on around you, you are still making a difference in the world.

Whether you own a million items or five, those possessions don't define who you really are. Yes, they may represent what you value, but they can only affect a limited part of who you are or what impact you have on other people.

Decluttering is a fairly long process. And while it seems like life is always hectic, there truly are seasons or days that are more overwhelming than others. It's okay to not always accomplish as much as we hoped. Obviously, I think accomplishment is great, but it's not where our worth comes from. So let's not give up when we have a rough day or week or year. The biggest and best change I've seen in regards to my clutter is how, little by little, it's still improving rather than going back to how it was.

We don't have to succeed constantly to be successful overall.

I know *I* didn't. But when I felt I wasn't succeeding, I'd grab hold of every tiny victory I could and hone in on the benefits each one gave me. I'd celebrate it and focus on the joy it was bringing me until it felt much bigger than it was. And soon it did become bigger.

The small victories added up, and I experienced more wins than losses. The momentum kept carrying me further.

I'm so glad to be able to truthfully tell you that it didn't take ten years nor perfect dedication for me to go from packrat to clutter-free. But it's even better to know that it hasn't changed my identity. I'm still that same, free-spirited girl I've always been.

My next step, after enjoying my uncluttered home with guests, was to use all that time I'd previously spent on decluttering for some other goal. That time has been able to go toward writing this book, taking care of my dad, and even getting married! I hadn't planned on doing any of these as my "project," but being done with the major decluttering has made it easier to pursue these other important ventures.

If a packrat like me can change, so can you. It doesn't matter your age. For some reason, I thought I'd be done making major changes to my habits by the time I was twenty-five. I'm so glad I didn't. And now I've been able to help people still in their first decade of life and others in their last. It doesn't matter if you were raised by a hoarder or a neat freak. I've heard from people raised by both extremes. Each person has their own journey.

Don't let any kind of fear keep you from taking the next step on your journey to a clutter-free life. Instead, set out to prove those fears wrong. You have what it takes to focus and accomplish this and make room for pursuing even bigger dreams. Your life will improve, and you'll impact others because of the changes you start making today.

QUIZ:
HOW CLUTTERED ARE YOU?

Grab a pencil. Then get comfy and ready to learn about yourself.

Do you have hoarding tendencies? Or are you more of a minimalist? Do you know you're a packrat and want to see how you compare to others? Take this short quiz to discover where you are on the clutter continuum.

Mark your answers here, so you can count up your score at the end.

Question #	1	2	3	4	5	6	7
My Answer							
Score							

Total Score _____

1. Complete this statement: If I continue with my current habits regarding possessions, I would consider myself a hoarder _____.

   A. in 10 years
   B. in 25 years
   C. in 50 years

D. never

2. True or false: I don't have time to think about what's most important to me each week, month, or year, much less come up with a plan to focus on what matters most.

    A. True
    B. False

3. How many boxes do you currently have in storage?

    A. More than I can count
    B. 0-5
    C. 6-10
    D. 11-20

4. Is there a room you put stuff in and close the door when company is over?

    A. No.
    B. Yes! You mean I'm not the only one?
    C. I have more than one room like that!
    D. I don't really have guests. Too many other things to do.

5. Do you like to organize but not get rid of stuff?

    A. Yes.
    B. I don't like either one.
    C. I like both.
    D. I like to get rid of stuff but not organize.

6. **Do you have items you want to sell but haven't yet?**
    A. No.
    B. Yes, about 1-5.
    C. Yes, lots of stuff.
    D. Yes, and it's taking over!

7. **Which of these statements are excuses you use for not getting rid of stuff?** (Choose all that apply.)

    A. I like my stuff and want to keep it.
    B. I might need it one day.
    C. I don't have time.
    D. I just need more space.
    E. It's not a priority; I have more important things to do.
    F. It'll just get cluttered again.
    G. My family or roommate doesn't help.

Score Key

Question 1:
A = 15
B = 10
C = 5
D = 0

Question 2:
A = 10
B = 0

Question 3:

A = 15
B = 0
C = 5
D = 10

Question 4:
A = 0
B = 5
C = 0
D = 15

Question 5:
A = 10
B = 15
C = 0
D = 5

Question 6:
A = 0
B = 5
C = 10
D = 15

Question 7: 5 points for each excuse you use

Add up your points and check the next page to see where you ended up.

Clutter Continuum

1 -- 10 -- 20 -- 30 -- 40 -- 50 -- 60 -- 70 -- 80 -- 90 -- 100 -- 110 -- 120

Almost Minimalist - - - - - - - - Packrat - - - - - - - Borderline Hoarder

0-40 Points
Almost Minimalist

You seem to be doing a pretty good job already. That doesn't mean you never struggle, but you probably know how to keep your possessions from taking over even though you might not always implement strategies for becoming clutter-free. While there may be room for improvement, remember that getting rid of stuff is about making room for what's important. Don't let having the bare minimum become more important than your relationships. And it's okay to have things you use and enjoy even if they aren't technically a *need*.

If this is you, start by helping others get rid of clutter. Review the guidelines in the chapter titled "What if I Don't have Time?" In doing this, you'll learn new tactics for your own life and stay motivated to prevent the chaos from building up in your home. Plus, your friend will benefit from your help!

40-80 Points
Packrat

Things could be worse, of course, but they could also be better. If you put a little effort into simplifying your life, you can develop habits that allow you to focus on people and activities you enjoy.

If this is you, start small. Too many people get overwhelmed by thinking of everything they need to do at once. Even if clothing isn't what's bothering you the most right now, start with that. It's very easy to break it down into even smaller chunks. First, get rid of any of your shirts that annoy you for whatever reason.

80-120 Points
Borderline Hoarder

There is still hope! It may take a lot of work, but it'll be worth it. If you decide to start cutting clutter from your life today, you will be so glad a year from now. By consistently making small changes that have a big impact, you will begin to notice a positive difference in your energy level, your relationships, your confidence, and even your wallet. Clutter may seem unimportant, but it influences every area of your life. Make getting rid of it a priority and your life will slowly transform, not because it's a magical formula but because it gives you time and space for what means the most to you.

If this is you, start by scheduling a time to declutter each week. You could declutter every day, depending on your schedule. Either way, look at your calendar now and block off 10-45 minutes to declutter. Set reminders for yourself to actually use that time to get rid of stuff. Then keep reading this book for more ideas and encouragement!

Make a Plan

Based on all you've learned, it's time to come up with your own plan for the next six months. What's realistic for you? Write a simple plan for each month similar to the one in the chapter called "It Matters Where You Start." Make it as easy on yourself to follow through as possible. Though my time as your guide through reading this book is ending, the words will stay in your heart and mind. Happy decluttering!

If you enjoyed *Packrat to Clutter-Free*, would you take a moment to:

Leave a review on Amazon. That's one of the **best** ways to help other people decide if this is a book they should read. You could share one of the stories or steps from this book that impacted you.

Text CLUTTER to 31996 to receive Tuesday Texts
with quotes to inspire simplicity!

(5msgs/month. Reply STOP to cancel, HELP for help. Msg&data rates may apply.)

A note from the author

Thank you for taking the time to read my book.

I love hearing from readers! It's what keeps me writing. I hope you'll share your decluttering accomplishments with me and let me know how they've transformed your life.

You can write to me at mcstarbuck@gmail.com with the subject Packrat to Clutter-Free.

I look forward to hearing from you!

Sincerely,

M.C. Starbuck

Coming Soon
from M. C. Starbuck

Whether single or married, too many people carry one or more of the top 5 fears of marriage: divorce, cheating, falling out of love, having a marriage like your parents, and the unknowns of how marriage will affect you. Letting go of fears and cynicism surrounding marriage doesn't have to be complicated. *Surprised by Marriage* shows readers how they can confidently enjoy the marriage they already have or will have in the future.

Sign up to receive **Fun & Fabulous** Friday emails at mcstarbuck.com

About the Author

M. C. Starbuck is a small-town girl turned world traveler. A few things that survived her year of decluttering: backpacking gear, handwritten letters and journals, and her Jane Austen collection. She writes about making room for what matters at LivingTinyDreamingBig.com.

Find her Quick-Start Guide to Publishing at mcstarbuck.com/how-to-be-a-writer

Acknowledgements

Special thanks to my amazing Mr. Darcy for supporting my goal of finishing this book and providing the tools for me to do just that. I'd still be struggling with it if not for you. I'm so lucky to have you in my life.

Thanks to my family and friends who have given me ideas for the book and encouraged me by being excited about all my endeavors.

Thanks to Pam Book for the idea of the subtitle and to Jeff Goins who inspires writers like me to get their first book published and gives practical advice for every stage of the process. And thank you, Jon Acuff, for giving me a structure for getting things done in a way that's manageable for me and for providing a group that motivated me to finally start a blog. Thank you, Joshua Becker, for sharing my article with your readers on *Becoming Minimalist*.

Thanks to my teachers throughout the years from elementary through college, who paved the way for me to achieve this dream. I appreciate the affirmation and guidance in the craft of writing.

Thank you a thousand times to everyone who helped with the editing process, making this book a work to be proud of: Candace Hall, Shannon Hammar, Heather Parady, Nick Spindler, Jennifer Navarre, Beverly Patrick, Susan Wetzel, Judi Hyvarinen, Jennifer Ullrich, Meaghan Rand Nix, and Jennifer Kim. I hope you know your worth. That goes for my Launch Team as well. This book would not have touched as many lives if it weren't for you.

Most importantly, may God receive all the credit for allowing me to live this life and for any good that my story brings to the lives of others. I pray I never forget to thank Him for everything, as He is the source of each blessing.

Made in the USA
Middletown, DE
02 July 2023

34369443R00094